AIRCAM/**AIRWAR** SERIES   EDITOR: MARTIN WINDROW

USAAF FIGHTER UNITS
EUROPE 1942-45

BY RENÉ J. FRANÇILLON

D1397955

COLOR PLATES BY
MICHAEL ROFFE AND
GERRY EMBLETON

SKY BOOKS PRESS

Published in 1977 by
Osprey Publishing Ltd
Member Company of the George Philip Group
12–14 Long Acre, London WC2E 9LP
Color plates © Copyright 1977 Osprey Publishing Ltd

Published in the USA 1977 by
Sky Books Press Ltd
48 East 50th Street
New York, NY 10022, USA

ISBN 0-89402-023-4 (Paper Edition)
ISBN 0-89402-024-2 (Cloth Edition)

Printed in Hong Kong

PRELUDE

The early thirties were lean years for the development of military aviation in the United States. Pacifism and isolationism were the prevailing sentiments among Americans of that time, and the Depression, which was weakening the American economy, caused severe budgetary limitations to be imposed. Procurements for the Army Air Corps, including experimental aircraft and trainers, dipped to only 115 aircraft in 1934 and averaged 476 aircraft per year during the thirties, before jumping to 3,162 aircraft in 1940 and 110,188 aircraft in 1942! Thus, in spite of the efforts of foresighted Air Corps officers, the role of this Service was being limited to air support of ground forces and to coastal defence. This situation was further consolidated by the findings of the Baker Board, which had been set up in 1934 to study the role of military aviation in the United States and which concluded that 'independent air missions have little effect upon the issue of battle and none upon the outcome of war'. Henceforth, limited budget allocations were used to maintain a small force capable of undertaking only these types of purely defensive operations.

Meanwhile, a very different atmosphere prevailed among the nations which were soon to become the Axis powers. In Italy General Giulio Douhet expounded his new strategic doctrine, calling for the need to secure air superiority, as, in his opinion, future wars would be won through power in the air. On the other side of the globe the Imperial Japanese Army and Navy, which fought a series of conflicts in China and Manchuria during the thirties, were steadily improving the qualitative and quantitative strength of their air arms, and were preparing to strike against Allied forces in south-east Asia and the Pacific. Perhaps even more threatening were developments taking place in Germany; Adolf Hitler became Chancellor of the Reich on 30 January 1933, and the Luftwaffe celebrated its official birth as an independent branch of the German armed forces during March 1935. Fortunately, during the same month, the United States Army organized the G.H.Q. Air Force, which did not come under the operational jurisdiction of the Air Corps and which, relieved of the responsibility for providing primary support for American ground forces, controlled American air striking forces. The stage for the great air operations of the Second World War was beginning to be set.

Though increasing emphasis was being placed by the G.H.Q. Air Force on independent strategic long-range operations, this was resisted within the War Department and, in May 1938, the Adjutant General informed the Assistant Secretary of War that 'the Chief of the Air Corps (General Oscar Westover) has been informed that the experimentation and development for the fiscal years 1939–40 (1 July 1938 through 30 June 1940) will be restricted to that class of aviation designed for the close-in support of ground troops and for the production of that type of aircraft such as medium and light bomber, pursuit and other light aircraft.' At the same time, the number of operational groups available to the Air Corps and the G.H.Q. Air Force was only increased from fifteen in early 1935 to sixteen in 1937; it was then held constant until 1 February 1940.

Events taking place in Europe and increased Japanese threats in south-east Asia and the Pacific finally led President F. D. Roosevelt to request in a message to Congress on 12 January 1939 that the Air Corps be expanded. The effectiveness of American military aviation was further strengthened on 20 June 1941 when Army Regulation 95-5 created the Army Air Force, combining the Air Corps and G.H.Q. Air Force under the authority of Maj. Gen. H. H. Arnold, who, as Chief of the Army Air Forces,

3

1. Curtiss P-40C of the 33rd Pursuit Squadron being loaded aboard the USS *Wasp* for transportation to Iceland in July 1941. This marked the initial deployment of US fighters to Europe and was part of America's attempt to gain a measure of control over the vital sea lanes across the Atlantic. (National Archives)

was directly responsible to the Army Chief of Staff.

At the same time that this expansion was taking place, the Roosevelt Administration implemented a new concept, 'Hemisphere Defense', and in March 1941 successfully negotiated with His Majesty's Government a 99-year lease on military bases to be located in Antigua, the Bahamas, Bermuda, British Guiana, Newfoundland, St Lucia and Trinidad. In April 1941 the United States obtained from the Danish Government-in-exile the rights to construct, maintain and operate landing fields in Greenland for the defence of this island. Finally, in July 1941, at the suggestion of the Icelandic Government, the United States agreed to supplement and eventually replace the British garrison in Iceland. By August 1941 the 33rd Pursuit Squadron of the Army Air Forces was operating from the Reykjavik aerodrome with 30 Curtiss P-40Cs. The Army Air Forces had arrived in Europe.

THE EVE OF WAR

In December 1941 the Army Air Forces had 71 operational groups: 27 Bombardment, 24 Pursuit,

4

11 Observation, 6 Transport, 2 Composite and 1 Photographic. One-third of the 24 Pursuit Groups (redesignated Fighter Groups in early 1942) were based outside the continental United States at the time of the Japanese attack in the Pacific: the 15th and 18th PGs were stationed in Hawaii, the 24th and 35th PGs were operating in the Philippines, the 16th, 32nd and 37th PGs were assigned to the defence of the Panama Canal Zone, and the 36th Pursuit Group operated from Losey Field, Puerto Rico. Of these units, only the 36th Pursuit (Fighter) Group served in the European Theatre of Operations (ETO) during the war. In addition, the 33rd Pursuit Squadron had been transferred out of the 8th Pursuit Group and assigned to the Iceland Base Command for operations from Reykjavik.

The remaining 16 Pursuit Groups were stationed in California (20th and 54th PGs at Hamilton Field, and 14th and 51st PGs at March Field), Connecticut (56th PG at Windsor Locks), Florida (53rd PG at MacDill Field and 49th PG at Morrison Field), Indiana (31st PG at Selfridge Field), Mississippi (50th PG at Key Field), New York (33rd PG at Mitchel Field), North Carolina (56th PG at Charlotte), Oregon (55th PG at Portland), and in Virginia (8th PG at Langley Field). One half of these units – the 1st, 14th, 20th, 31st, 50th, 52nd, 55th and 56th – were assigned to the ETO during the war but, perhaps more importantly, these prewar groups provided the cadres that were to lead the 37 fighter groups which, at one time or another, were assigned to the Eighth and Ninth Air Forces for operations in Northern Europe.

With the exception of the 1st and 14th Pursuit Groups, which were partially equipped with early Lockheed P-38 Lightnings but were not yet ready for combat, the fighter units of the Army Air Forces were flying obsolete, obsolescent or generally unsatisfactory aircraft. The most common type was the Curtiss P-40 Warhawk, including obsolescent P-40s, P-40Bs and P-40Cs as well as more modern P-40Ds and P-40Es. These were supplemented by a motley collection of Seversky P-35s, Curtiss P-36s, Bell P-39s and even antiquated Boeing P-26s. Two of these types, the Bell P-39 and Curtiss P-40, had by then been used in combat by the Royal Air Force,

2. Whereas the P-40C seen loaded aboard the USS *Wasp* bears the style of national markings adopted in 1941, which added a white star with red centre and blue background on each side of the fuselage, other aircraft of the 33rd Pursuit Squadron – as illustrated by the one seen here on take-off from the carrier – retained the full prewar standard of markings without national insignia on the fuselage. In its place the aircraft illustrated carried its squadron insignia. (National Archives)

the former proving to be an almost catastrophic failure when briefly flown from England by No. 601 Squadron. The latter, known to the RAF as the Tomahawk, in its early versions and as the Kittyhawk in its improved form, was operated with conspicuous success by squadrons in the Western Desert. UK-based units, however, used Tomahawks in the army co-operation role, as their Allison engine failed to confer the high-altitude performance necessary for fighter operations in Northern Europe. The obsolescent Curtiss Mohawk, the export version of the USAAF's P-36, had been found by the RAF to lack the performance necessary for operations against the Luftwaffe, and was therefore operated by the RAF exclusively in India. Finally, the Boeing P-26s and Seversky P-35s were clearly obsolete though they were briefly flown in combat in the Philippines. Thus, for the forthcoming operations against the Luftwaffe in Northern Europe, the USAAF could only count on two of the fighter types it had in service in December 1941, the P-38 Lightning and the P-39 Airacobra, of which

3. As insufficient numbers of US fighters with adequate performance were available at the time of America's entry into the war, three fighter groups of the Eighth Air Force were equipped with the Supermarine Spitfire Vb prior to commencing combat operations from bases in England. This wartime propaganda photograph is purported to show pilots of the 309th Fighter Squadron, 31st Fighter Group, 'scrambling'. (NA&SM)

combat-worthy versions were expected to become available in early 1942. By that time, however, the USAAF already had on order, or under test, a number of totally new fighter designs which owed much to European combat experience and one of these types, the Republic P-47 Thunderbolt, which had made its first flight on 6 May 1941 and was first delivered to the 56th Fighter Group during June 1942, became the mainstay of the USAAF fighter operations in the ETO. Furthermore, the USAAF fortuitously acquired in 1943 another type of fighter aircraft, the Rolls-Royce Merlin-powered North American P-51 Mustang, which during the last year of the war reigned supreme over Northern Europe.

NORTHERN EUROPE

On 22 December 1941, three weeks after the United States had been forced into World War II by Japanese aggression, Prime Minister Churchill arrived in Washington DC aboard HMS *Duke of York*. During meetings which then took place between President Roosevelt, Prime Minister Churchill and their staffs, the leaders of the Western Allies agreed that the war effort against Germany was to take priority over the fight against Japan as soon as alarming Japanese advances could be checked. As part of this strategy, the United States was to establish as soon as feasible an Army Air Force in Great Britain to mount a strategic offensive against industrial targets in Germany and occupied Europe. The Eighth Air Force, as the UK-based component of the USAAF became known in April 1942, was scheduled to include primarily Bombardment (Heavy) and Fighter Groups as well as some Bombardment (Medium), Reconnaissance and Troop Carrier Groups plus support units.

Five fighter groups were initially selected for assignment to the Eighth Air Force; these included the 1st and 14th FGs with Lockheed P-38Fs, the 31st and 52nd FGs which were to be equipped with Bell P-39Fs, and the 4th Fighter Group, which was to be formed in England by incorporating into the USAAF three RAF squadrons (Nos. 71, 121 and 133) manned by American volunteers and equipped with Supermarine Spitfires. The most urgent problem for the four groups in the United States was to get their aircraft quickly and safely to England, as the submarines of the Kriegsmarine were on the verge of winning the Battle of the Atlantic, which made the shipping of precious fighter aircraft a very costly and sometimes ineffective venture. Consequently, as Lockheed had developed 165 gal (625 litre) drop tanks which, when two were carried, gave the P-38F a range with reserves of 1,700 miles (2,735 km), it was decided to ferry the Lightnings of the 1st and 14th Fighter Groups from the United States to England. After a number of postponements, brought about by delays in the production of drop tanks and by the need to retain the fighters in the United States until the American victory at Midway had eliminated the Japanese threat against the West Coast, the ferry flights got underway in June 1942 under the name of Operation *Bolero*. The first P-38Fs arrived in Scotland in July after flying the 2,965 mile (4,770 km) route from Presque Isle, Maine to Prestwick, via Goose Bay, Bluie West 1 and Reykjavik. Meanwhile, it had been decided that the

P-39 was not fitted for combat operations in Northern Europe, and personnel from the 31st and 52nd Fighter Groups were sent to England without aircraft, as these two units were to be re-equipped with 200 Supermarine Spitfire Mk Vbs supplied by Great Britain under reverse lend-lease.

Whilst on its way to England the 27th Fighter Squadron of the 1st Fighter Group was held back in Iceland to assist the 33rd Fighter Squadron – the USAAF unit which in August 1941 had been assigned to the Iceland Base Command – to fly defensive patrols over the vital island base in the middle of the Atlantic. Even though the pilots of the 27th FS were eager to reach England to begin combat operations and disappointed by this delay, the temporary assignment to Iceland proved to be a lucky one. On 14 August 1942, 2nd Lt. Elza Shahan flying a P-38F of the 27th FS shared with 2nd Lt. Joseph Shaffer, who flew a P-40C of the 33rd FS, in the destruction of a Fw200C-3 to obtain the USAAF's first victory against the Luftwaffe.

The first USAAF fighter unit to begin combat operations from an English base was the Spitfire-equipped 31st FG which, after some of its pilots had flown sorties with the RAF, mounted its first squadron-strength mission on 5 August 1942 and was fully operational two weeks later when 2nd Lt.

4. Using the Spitfire Vbs obtained under reverse lend-lease, the 31st Fighter Group became the Eighth Air Force's first group to commence operations. Sorties were flown with the RAF beginning on 26 July 1942 and first squadron-strength operations took place on 5 August. However, in the autumn of 1942, the 31st FG and its Spitfires were transferred to the Twelfth Air Force for operations in North Africa. (NA&SM)

5. Equipped with P-38Hs, the 55th FG became the third Lightning group of the Eighth Air Force to enter combat when, operating from Nuthampstead, it flew its first mission on 15 October 1943. The three aircraft illustrated belonged to the 338th Fighter Squadron and were photographed on 12 December 1943 at Bassingbourne at the start of an escort mission. (USAF)

Sam Junkins shot down a Fw190A whilst the 31st was flying in support of the landing operations at Dieppe. Following the same pattern, pilots of the 52nd FG flew combat sorties with the RAF and the Group's 2nd and 4th Fighter Squadrons began flying squadron-strength missions before the end of August 1942. The two Lightning groups, the 1st and 14th FGs, were unable to enter combat until their aircraft had been fitted with VHF radio equipment compatible with that being used by the RAF; minor technical problems and the necessity to train their pilots under operational conditions also delayed them. Thus, after flying some defensive sorties in late August 1942, the 1st FG flew the first P-38 mission in the ETO on 2 September 1942. A month later, the 14th FG went operational. However, by then the Eighth Air Force had already been notified that its first four fighter units, as well as some of its B-17s and transports, were to be transferred to the newly formed Twelfth Air Force for operations in support of Operation *Torch*, the Allied invasion of North Africa in November 1942. The loss of these units was partially made up by the transfer to USAAF command of the three veteran RAF 'Eagle' squadrons, Nos. 71, 121 and 133, which on 29

6. **P-38Js of the 38th Fighter Squadron, 55th FG, became on 3 March 1944 the first Allied fighters to fly over Berlin. The long flight to the German capital was made possible by the use of two 150 US gallon tanks which increased total petrol capacity by almost 75 per cent. (Australian War Memorial).**

September 1942 became respectively the 334th, 335th and 336th Fighter Squadrons of the 4th Fighter Group. The 4th FG flew its first combat mission on 2 October 1942 and, from later in that month when the 1st, 14th, 31st and 52nd FGs joined the Twelfth Air Force until 13 April 1943 when the 56th and 78th FGs became operational, it continued to use RAF operational procedures, and flew most of its early missions, primarily cross-Channel fighter sweeps and escort of RAF Boston light bombers, under Fighter Command control. In the spring of 1943 the situation changed as, at long last, the Eighth Air Force received the fighter groups and aircraft it needed to perform its assigned task: daylight strategic bombing with fighter escort.

VIII FIGHTER COMMAND

The transfer of the 1st and 14th FGs to the Twelfth Air Force was a major setback for the Eighth Air Force which, for almost a year, was unable to obtain new Lightning groups, as P-38s were being assigned first to the North Africa and New Guinea/Solomons areas to offset attrition in existing groups, and to equip new units in these theatres. Furthermore, the limited number of Spitfires which were obtained under lend-lease were needed by the 4th FG of the Eighth Air Force and by fighter groups of the Twelfth Air Force. The only other type of US fighter with sufficient performance for operations in Northern Europe, the Republic P-47 Thunderbolt, was suffering more than its share of teething troubles and was not available in sufficient numbers until early in 1943.

The first Thunderbolts for the Eighth Air Force had been shipped to England in December 1942. In addition to being used for re-equipping the 4th FG, P-47Cs were assigned to the 56th FG, which had trained in America on P-47Bs, and to the 78th FG, which had been scheduled to begin combat operations with Lightnings but which, shortly after arriving in England, had been stripped of its aircraft and of most of its pilots in order to make up attrition in P-38 units operating in North Africa. Even

though its pilots were less than thrilled to exchange their beloved Spitfires for faster but heavier Thunderbolts, the battle-tested 4th FG was selected to make the combat debut of the P-47 as soon as the aircraft could be suitably modified and fitted with the necessary VHF radio equipment. Thus, on 8 April 1943 the 4th FG, together with one flight each from the 56th and 78th FGs, took 24 P-47Cs on an uneventful mission from Debden over the Pas de Calais. Missions flown during the next few days, in which an increasing number of pilots from the two new groups joined the veterans of the 4th FG, failed to result in contact with the Luftwaffe and were marred by several engine failures. However, on 15 April, 60 Thunderbolts from all three groups finally came to grips with German fighters, and three Fw190s were shot down for the loss of an equal

7. These P-38Js of the 38th Fighter Squadron, 55th Fighter Group, illustrate the squadron identification markings – a triangle on the outside of each vertical tail surface – adopted during December 1943 to facilitate inflight recognition of each squadron. Thus, the two other squadrons of the 55th FG used a circle (338th) and a square (343rd). The aircraft's individual letter – in the case of these three aircraft H, U and I – were applied on the outside of each radiator fairing and repeated on the inside of each vertical tail surface. (USAF)

number of P-47s (one of which was due to enemy action and the other two to engine failure).

The initial unreliability of the Pratt & Whitney R-2800 engine powering the Thunderbolt and the need to train the pilots of the 56th and 78th FGs under combat conditions restricted the use of the P-47 to fighter sweeps until 4 May when the 4th and 56th FGs escorted B-17s to Antwerp whilst the 78th

8. Lockheed P-38J-15-LO (43-28474) of the 434th Fighter Squadron, 479th Fighter Group, coming in for a landing with full flaps down. This photograph was taken during the summer of 1944 shortly after 29 July when Captain Jeffrey of the 479th FG had become the first pilot to engage a jet aircraft. Less than two months later this group converted to P-51Ds. (USAF)

flew a diversionary mission to Paris. Initial combat experience confirmed results obtained during tests against captured enemy aircraft and indicated that the P-47 had superior performance above 20,000 ft (6,096 m) but that at lower altitudes it was inferior to German fighters; the major shortcoming of the first combat-worthy P-47s was their insufficient range which, albeit slightly better than that of Spitfires, prevented them from escorting bombers on deep penetration missions. Accordingly, priority was given by the Air Technical Section of VIII Fighter Command to devising means to extend the range of the Thunderbolt. To that effect a number of drop-tank designs were evaluated, and two models of tanks to be carried beneath the fuselage were retained for long-range use, a 75 gal (284 litre) metal tank and a 108 gal (409 litre) paper tank. In addition, beginning with aircraft in the P-47D-15-RE and -15-RA blocks, Republic delivered aircraft fitted with wing racks which could be adapted to carry either drop tanks or bombs. Using ventral drop tanks, Thunderbolts began flying missions over Germany on 30 August 1943 and, four weeks later, the 4th, 56th, 78th and 353rd FGs escorted bombers all the way to and from a target in Germany. At long last

the Eighth Air Force had a fighter capable of providing proper escort for its bombers.

Whilst long-range fighter operations were being developed by the pioneer P-47 groups, the Eighth Air Force was being built up, and, between August and December 1943, six Thunderbolt-equipped fighter groups – the 352nd, 353rd, 355th, 356th, 358th and 359th – began operations. In addition, the 20th and 55th FGs, which were then flying P-38Hs, became operational on 28 December and 15 October 1943, respectively. Thus, whereas a year earlier it only had one fighter group in operation (the Spitfire-equipped 4th FG), the Eighth Air Force had at the end of 1943 nine P-47 and two P-38 groups to escort the B-17s and B-24s of its twenty-two Bombardment Groups (Heavy). The effectiveness of fighter-escort operations was demonstrated both by mounting scores – the 56th FG becoming on 5 November 1943 the first Eighth Air Force unit to be credited with 100 enemy aircraft destroyed – and by the marked reduction in bomber losses. Encouraging as they were, these results were to be far surpassed during the following year when the Luftwaffe was forced to assign an ever increasing share of its fighter force to the defence of the Reich and thus could not effectively support the Wehrmacht operations in Italy, France and Eastern Europe.

FESTUNG EUROPA PENETRATED

Taking advantage of their better performance at high altitude, the Thunderbolts of the Eighth Air Force usually flew above the heavy bomber formations. From their high position the P-47s were then able to dive on the attacking German fighters which were instructed to avoid engaging the escorting fighters and to concentrate on the bombers. These tactics employed by the Eighth Air Force fighters often succeeded in breaking up concentrated attacks by the Luftwaffe. Moreover, the Thunderbolts and Lightnings were able to provide effective protection for crippled bombers straggling behind the main formations and which, until the advent of adequate fighter cover, had proved easy prey for the Luftwaffe.

In planning 1944 operations in Northern Europe, the USAAF had intended to equip most of the fighter groups of the Eighth Air Force with Thunderbolts, with a few groups being scheduled to fly Lightnings, whilst the newly created Ninth Air Force was to have its fighter groups equipped mainly with the new Merlin-powered Mustangs. However, when on 1 December 1943 the 354th FG of the Ninth Air Force took the P-51B into combat, it was led by Lt. Col. Blakeslee of the 4th FG and it operated under Eighth Air Force control. Immediately the Mustang proved itself to be the ideal escort fighter, combining speed, manoeuvrability and range, and it became a remarkably successful weapon. The Thunderbolt had already proved itself to be a most effective fighter bomber, capable of absorbing considerable AA damage and of delivering a very heavy punch, but it was not without much heated argument that the Eighth and Ninth Air Forces agreed to trade Mustangs for Thunderbolts.

The first step in implementing this plan consisted of the exchange of the P-47-equipped 358th FG, which had become operational with the Eighth Air Force on 20 December 1943, for the 357th FG which, equipped with P-51Bs, had been initially assigned to the Ninth Air Force but began combat operations on 11 February 1944 as an Eighth Air Force unit. During the latter part of that month, the 4th FG became the first Eighth Air Force unit to be re-equipped with Mustangs. The following ten months saw seven other P-47 groups (the 78th, 352nd, 353rd, 355th, 356th, 359th and 361st FGs) and four P-38 groups (the 20th, 55th, 364th and 479th FGs) converted to Mustangs, leaving the 56th FG as the only Eighth Air Force combat group to fly Thunderbolts, including the rare P-47M version, until VE-Day. As was apparent from the unit designations listed, the Eighth Air Force had also reached its peak fighter strength of fifteen groups during this period when, on 26 May 1944, the P-38J-equipped 479th FG had become the last Eighth Air Force fighter group to commence combat operations.

At the same time as its fighter groups were being

9. Capable of lifting over short tactical ranges a bombload equal to that of medium bombers, the Lightning lacked, in its standard single-seater form, the ability to bomb accurately whilst flying level. To remedy this deficiency and take advantage of the aircraft's load-carrying capability, a 'drop-snoot' version of the P-38J and P-38L was developed and was characterized by a revised nose configuration in which the forward-firing guns were replaced by a bomb-aimer station complete with second seat and Norden bombsight. (USAF)

re-equipped, the Eighth Air Force increased the tempo of its escort operations and began flying deeper into Europe, capitalizing on the increased range of its later model P-47s, P-38s and P-51s,

10. Close-up details of the bombardier position and Allison V-1710-89 and -91 engines of a 'drop-snoot' P-38J. The bombracks beneath the inner wing panels could each carry bombs of up to 2,000 lb. (USAF)

which were all now fitted to carry two wing drop tanks. The distinction of being the first Allied fighter aircraft to fly over Berlin was gained on 3 March 1944 by P-38Js of the 55th FG led by Lt. Col. Jack Jenkins; on the following day Mustangs of the 4th, 354th, 357th and 363rd FGs (the latter unit was assigned to the Ninth Air Force but, for the occasion, was operating under VIII Fighter Command control) became the first USAAF fighters to engage the Luftwaffe over the German capital. Unfortunately, on that day the Mustangs did not live up to their already great reputation, as eight P-51s were shot down whilst fifteen more Mustangs were lost due to engine problems and appalling weather conditions; the P-51s, however, claimed the destruction of eight German aircraft. Another type of long-range operation was pioneered between 21 June and 5 July 1944, when 67 P-51s of the 4th and 352nd FGs flew the first shuttle mission between England, Russia, Italy and back to England to escort B-17s.

Whether operating on the more spectacular missions, such as those to Berlin and to Russia, or escorting the heavies to an ever increasing number of other targets, the Mustangs, Thunderbolts and Lightnings of the Eighth Air Force took a mounting toll of the Luftwaffe units defending the Third Reich. In the process, 261 pilots shot down five or more enemy aircraft and amongst these aces the following pilots were credited with the destruction in air combat of twenty or more German aircraft:

Pilot's name and last rank during the war	No. of enemy a/c destroyed in the air	Unit	Types of a/c flown in combat	Fate
Lt. Col. Francis S. Gabreski	28	56th FG	P-47	P.O.W.
Maj. Robert S. Johnson	28	56th FG	P-47	
Maj. George E. Preddy	26.83	352nd FG	P-47/P-51	K.I.A.
Lt. Col. John C. Meyer	24	352nd FG	P-47/P-51	
Maj. Ray. S. Wetmore	22.60	359th FG	P-47/P-51	
Lt. Col. David C. Schilling	22.50	56th FG	P-47	
Capt. Don S. Gentile	21.80	133 Sqn & 4th FG	Spitfire P-47/P-51	
1st Lt. Fred J. Christensen	21.50	56th FG	P-47	
Maj. Walker H. Mahurin	20.75	56th FG	P-47	

TACTICAL OPERATIONS

Though the escort missions flown by the Eighth Air Force are better remembered, more sorties were in fact flown in Northern Europe by USAAF fighters performing other fighter operations such as train busting, airfield strafing, tactical air support and interdiction. These types of operations were pioneered in the ETO by Lt. Quince L. Brown of the 78th FG who, on 30 July 1943, had gone down on the deck to strafe a locomotive and a gun position after returning from an escort mission. By early 1944 the practice of attacking targets of opportunity on the ground or at low altitude, was becoming more common and VIII Fighter Command, recognizing the high risks involved in shooting up well-defended targets such as airfields, began counting the destruction of enemy aircraft on the ground on par with air victories. But, in spite of the specialized tactics developed in March and April 1944 by the 353rd FG, losses incurred by the US fighters were fairly high; the results achieved, however, were judged to be more than worth the additional losses. Four pilots of the Eighth Air Force were credited with 20 or more enemy aircraft destroyed on the ground: Lt. Col. Elwyn G. Righetti (27 on the ground and 7.5 in the air), Lt. Col. Joseph L. Thury (25 and 2.5), 1st Lt. William J. Cullerton (21 and 6) and Lt. Col. John D. Landers (20 and 8.5).

In addition to developing airfield-strafing tactics, the 353rd FG pioneered dive-bombing operations

in Northern Europe; 500 lb (227 kg) bombs were carried by P47 Thunderbolts for the first time on 25 November 1943 and 1,000 lb (454 kg) bombs on wing shackles were first carried on 15 March 1944. On the 10th of the following month the Lightnings of the 20th and 55th FGs were initiated as fighter bombers when, led by specially devised 'Droop Snoot' P-38Js incorporating a bombardier station in the nose, they successfully bombed and strafed airfields at St Dizier, France, and Gutersloh, Germany. Strafing and bombing operations were carried out by all three types of Eighth Air Force fighter until VE-Day as an adjunct to their primary bomber escort missions, but fighter bomber operations were the main task for the fighter groups of the Ninth Air Force.

First operating in the Western Desert between November 1942 and August 1943, the Ninth Air Force was re-established in England on 16 October 1943 to provide tactical air support for the ground forces which were soon to land in France. Its first fighter unit was the Mustang-equipped 354th FG which, as related earlier, flew its first mission on 1 December 1943 under the control of VIII Fighter Command. During the following six months the

11. 42-68701, a P-38J-10-LO of the 367th FG, Ninth Air Force, which made the first landing in liberated France when technical troubles forced it down at ELS-1, Emergency Landing Strip One, Poupeville. Part of the supply fleet supporting the Normandy landings can be seen in the background. (USAF)

strength of the Ninth Air Force was rapidly built up and, in accordance with the agreement reached with the Eighth Air Force, the Thunderbolt was to become its main fighter type. Thus, when on 9 May 1944 the 406th FG became operational and brought the Ninth Air Force to its peak strength, there were thirteen groups equipped with P-47s (the 36th, 48th, 50th, 358th, 362nd, 365th, 366th, 368th, 371st, 373rd, 404th, 405th and 406th FGs), three with P-38s (the 367th, 370th and 474th FGs), and two with P-51s (the 354th and 363rd FGs). In time, the 367th exchanged its Lightnings for Thunderbolts and the 370th was re-equipped with Mustangs whilst the 363rd FG was redesignated as the 363rd Tactical Reconnaissance Group and the 354th FG, the Pioneer Mustang Group, briefly operated P-47s during the winter of 1944–45 prior to being equipped again with P-51s.

13

12. Framed by the starboard boom of another Lightning, a P-38J of the 479th FG is seen warming up its engine prior to taking off for a bomber escort mission to Germany. This group, named the 'Riddle's Raiders' after its first CO – Lt. Col. Kyle L. Riddle – was stationed at Wattisham during its single year of operations in the ETO. (USAF)

Even though some of the fighter groups of the Ninth Air Force, notably the Mustang-equipped 354th and 363rd FGs, assisted the Eighth Air Force in early 1944 by flying bomber escort missions, these units were intended to operate in the tactical role. Thus, in preparation for the impending landing in Normandy, the fighters of the Ninth Air Force mounted an intensive interdiction campaign to create havoc in the German ground transportation system in occupied Europe. Then, on 6 June 1944, the Ninth Air Force was called upon to perform the type of mission it had been organized for; Allied troops had landed in Normandy and were battling with the Wehrmacht in the last phase of the war. After providing support to the landing forces from their bases in England, the fighter groups of the Ninth Air Force, reinforced by some of the Eighth Air Force groups, which were temporarily assigned a tactical role, moved to bases on the Continent from where they could provide quicker reaction calls for help from hard-pressed ground units. To perform these missions the Ninth Air Force organized three specialized commands: the IX Tactical Air Command, which operated primarily in support of the US First Army, the XIX Tactical Air Command, which worked mainly with

the US Third Army, and the XXIX Tactical Air Command, which supported the US Seventh Army, to which groups were assigned as required. Later, the First Tactical Air Force (Provisional) was formed to support the French First Army and was made up of units coming from the Ninth and Twelfth Air Forces and from the French First Air Force. The effectiveness of these fighter bomber operations was always apparent, but it was demonstrated particularly brilliantly during the closing of the Falaise gap when the Wehrmacht suffered heavy losses from co-ordinated air attacks, and during the Battle of the Bulge when, as soon as the weather cleared enough to permit resumption of air operations, the Ninth Air Force broke the back of the last German offensive of the war.

Whereas the bulk of the fighter strength of the Ninth Air Force was made up of Thunderbolts, Lightnings and Mustangs, this air force also operated two independent squadrons, the 422nd and 425th Night Fighter Squadrons, which were equipped with twin-engined Northrop P-61 Black Widows. The first of these units to arrive in the ETO was the 422nd NFS which reached England, without its aircraft, in March 1944 and received its first P-61A-5-NO less than two months later. After receiving some operational training with the RAF, the unit flew its first anti-diver sortie (interception of V-1 buzz bombs) from Ford, Sussex during the night of 15 July, and it destroyed its first V-1 during the following night. In late July 1944 the 422nd NFS moved to the Continent to be based initially at Mauperthuis, France; it was from this base that Lt. Smith (pilot) and Lt. Tierney (radar operator) flew to obtain the first P-61 victory when, on 7 August 1944, they teamed to shoot down a Bf110. In France the 422nd was joined by the 425th NFS and the two squadrons provided night defence for American ground forces until VE-Day. They also flew an increasing number of night interdiction sorties in which they put to good use the four 20mm forward-firing cannon of their Black Widows as well as the external load of bombs, napalm and rockets which their aircraft were adapted to carry.

Though the fighter groups of the Ninth Air Force were assigned primarily a tactical mission, and thus

14

had fewer opportunities to encounter the Luftwaffe in the air than the units of the Eighth Air Force flying primarily in the escort role, they none the less produced 68 aces. Three of them – Maj. Clyde B. East (12 victories), Capt. John H. Hoefker (8.5 victories) and Lt. Leland A. Larson (6 victories) – were not even assigned to fighter groups, and they scored against the Luftwaffe whilst flying F-6s (the armed reconnaissance version of the Mustang) with the 10th Photographic Reconnaissance Group; the pilot/radar-operator teams of Lts. Paul A. Smith/Robert E. Tierney and of Lts. Herman Ernst/Edward Kopsel became the first two American team aces as members of the P-61 equipped 422nd Night Fighter Squadron. The top ranking ace of the Ninth Air Force was Lt. Col. Glenn T. Eagleston who was credited with the destruction in the air of 18.5 enemy aircraft.

13. Named 'Kokomo' this P-47D-25-RE (42-26637) was the personal aircraft of Maj. General William E. Kepner who, in March 1945 when this photograph was taken, was CO of the 2nd Air Division, Eighth Air Force. (USAF)

FIGHTER GROUPS IN EUROPE, 1942-45

Eighth Air Force

1st FIGHTER GROUP

Tracing its ancestry back to the original 1st Pursuit Group, which had been organized in France on 5 May 1918 as a part of the Air Service, A.E.F. (American Expeditionary Force), the 1st Fighter Group flew its P-38Fs across the Atlantic with the first aircraft leaving the United States (Presque Isle,

Maine) on 23 June 1942. Whilst in transit to England one of the three squadrons, the 27th Fighter Squadron, of the 1st FG was retained in Iceland until late August to provide air defence for the American base at Reykjavik whereas the other two squadrons, the 71st and the 94th, proceed to their destination.

On 29 August 1942 P-38Fs of the 94th Fighter Squadron flew the first air defence sorties from Ibsley, Hants, and the group's first offensive mission was flown on 2 September. However, less than eight weeks later the 1st FG was transferred from the Eighth to the Twelfth Air Force for operations in North Africa. The codes HV, LM and UN, which had been assigned to the 27th, 71st and 94th Fighter squadrons, were retained upon the transfer of the 1st FG to North Africa and, within the Eighth Air Force, these codes were later assigned again respectively to the 61st, 62nd and 63rd Fighter Squadrons of the 56th FG.

4th FIGHTER GROUP

Proudly adopting the motto 'Fourth but First', the 4th FG was activated at Bushey Hall, Herts., England, when Nos. 71, 121, and 133 Sqns, RAF, were transferred to the USAAF. Manned by American volunteers, these 'Eagle' squadrons had served in the Royal Air Force since 5 February 1941

FIGHTER GROUPS AND THEIR AIRCRAFT, 8TH AIR FORCE, 1942–45

KEY: (−) Spitfire; (+) P-38; (=) P-47; (*) P-51

Unit	1942						1943												1944												1945				
	J	A	S	O	N	D	J	F	M	A	M	J	J	A	S	O	N	D	J	F	M	A	M	J	J	A	S	O	N	D	J	F	M	A	M
1st FG		+	+	+	to 12th AF																														
4th FG			—	—	—	—	—	—	=	=	=	=	=	=	=	=	=	=	=	*	*	*	*	*	*	*	*	*	*	*	*	*	*	*	*
14th FG				+	to 12th AF																														
20th FG																				+	+	+	+	+	+	+	*	*	*	*	*	*	*	*	*
31st FG			—	to 12th AF																															
52nd FG			—	to 12th AF																															
55th FG																		+	+	+	+	+	+	+	+	+	*	*	*	*	*	*	*	*	*
56th FG									=	=	=	=	=	=	=	=	=	=	=	=	=	=	=	=	=	=	=	=	=	=	=	=	=	=	=
78th FG	Arrived Dec. '42 with P-38 but no ops. with type									=	=	=	=	=	=	=	=	=	=	=	=	=	=	=	=	=	=	=	=	=	*	*	*	*	*
339th FG																			*	*	*	*	*	*	*	*	*	*	*	*	*	*	*	*	*
352nd FG												=	=	=	=	=	=	=	*	*	*	*	*	*	*	*	*	*	*	*	*	*	*	*	*
353rd FG									=	=	=	=	=	=	=	=	=	=	=	=	=	=	=	=	=	=	=	=	*	*	*	*	*	*	*
355th FG											=	=	=	=	=	=	=	*	*	*	*	*	*	*	*	*	*	*	*	*	*	*	*	*	*
356th FG											=	=	=	=	=	=	=	=	=	=	=	=	=	=	=	=	=	=	*	*	*	*	*	*	*
357th FG																			*	*	*	*	*	*	*	*	*	*	*	*	*	*	*	*	*
358th FG																		=	=	to 9th AF															
359th FG												=	=	=	=	=	=	=	*	*	*	*	*	*	*	*	*	*	*	*	*	*	*	*	*
361st FG													=	=	=	=	=	=	*	*	*	*	*	*	*	*	*	*	*	*	*	*	*	*	*
364th FG																						+	+	+	+	*	*	*	*	*	*	*	*	*	*
479th FG																									+	+	+	+	*	*	*	*	*	*	*
Spitfire groups	0	2	2	2	1	1	1	1	0	0	0	0	0	0	0	0	0	0	0	0	2	0	0	0	0	0	0	0	0	0	0	0	0	0	0
P-38 groups	0	1	1	2	0	0	0	0	0	0	0	0	0	0	0	0	0	1	1	2	2	2	3	3	4	4	1	1	0	0	0	0	0	0	0
P-47 groups	0	0	0	0	0	0	0	0	1	3	3	3	3	4	6	7	7	9	10	8	7	6	4	4	4	4	4	3	2	2	1	1	1	1	1
P-51 groups	0	0	0	0	0	0	0	0	0	0	0	0	0	0	0	0	0	0	0	0	2	3	5	7	7	10	10	11	12	13	13	14	14	14	14
Total no. of groups	0	3	3	4	1	1	1	1	1	3	3	3	3	4	6	8	8	11	12	12	13	14	15	15	15	15	15	15	15	15	15	15	15	15	15

when No. 71 Sqn had flown its first operational patrol with Hawker Hurricane Is. Upon being transferred to the USAAF the three squadrons were renumbered 334th, 335th and 336th Fighter Squadrons but retained their Spitfire Vbs with codes XR, AV and MD.

As a unit of the Eighth Air Force the 4th FG flew its first mission from Debden, Essex – its base until VE-Day – on 2 October 1942. Its Spitfire Vbs were replaced by Thunderbolts (P-47Cs and then P-47Ds) in March 1943 but in February 1944 Merlin-powered aircraft were returned to the 4th FG when it was re-equipped with Mustangs.

With 583.5 enemy aircraft shot down and 469 aircraft destroyed on the ground, the 4th FG was the top-scoring USAAF fighter group and it also obtained the distinctions of being the first US fighter unit to penetrate the German air space and to engage enemy aircraft over both Paris and Berlin. It also won a DUC (Distinguished Unit Citation) for operations between 5 March and 24 April 1944 when it claimed the destruction of 189 aircraft in the air and 134 on the ground.

14th FIGHTER GROUP

Activated at Hamilton Field, California, on 15 January 1941, the 14th FG joined the 1st FG in ferrying its own P-38Fs to England in the early summer of 1942. Stationed at Atcham, Salop, the unit had been assigned to the Eighth Air Force; but, while still undergoing operational training, the 14th FG was re-assigned to the Twelfth Air Force on 14 September 1942. A few sweeps were flown from England under RAF guidance during the first three weeks of October prior to the group's departure for North Africa. Only two of the 14th FG's three squadrons, the 48th and 49th Fighter Squadrons, did take part in operations with the Eighth Air Force and their Lightnings bore the code letters ES and QU, respectively.

20th FIGHTER GROUP

This unit was the only prewar Army Air Corps group to serve with the Eighth Air Force for an extended period. It had been activated at Mather Field, California, on 15 November 1930 and was

14. 'Miss Carriage', a P-47D-25-RE, photographed in England on 23 November 1944. Note large star-and-bar national insignia beneath port wing of this aircraft, a marking peculiar to Thunderbolts operating in the ETO which was applied to prevent the radial-engined P-47 from being confused with the German Fw190. (Robert Baseler)

retained on the United States west coast until the summer of 1943 when it moved to Kings Cliffe, Northants. Following a number of squadron-strength missions when its 55th, 77th and 79th Fighter Squadrons (respectively coded KI, LC and MC) flew with the 55th Fighter Group, the 20th FG

15. War-weary P-47D-5-RE with Malcolm hood assigned as a monitor aircraft to the 491st Bombardment Group. The original Olive Drab/Neutral Gray camouflage has been removed and the cowling and vertical tail surfaces have been painted with green and white bands; the aircraft letter T in the white tail band was also painted green. (USAF)

only DUC was won on 8 April 1944 when its Lightnings flew a very successful fighter sweep against airfields and other ground targets in the vicinity of Salzwedel, 80 miles west of Berlin.

31st FIGHTER GROUP

First unit to be equipped with the unique Bell P-39 Airacobra, the 31st FG had been activated at Selfridge Field, Michigan, on 1 February 1940 and had been scheduled to fly P-39Fs across the Atlantic to join the Eighth Air Force during the summer of 1942. However, as the P-39 was found unsuitable for operations in the ETO, the group's personnel moved to England, without aircraft, to be equipped with Spitfire Vbs obtained under reverse lend-lease. A number of sorties were flown with the RAF by pilots and aircraft of the 31st FG beginning 26 July 1942 and the first group-strength mission was flown on 29 August 1942 to establish the 31st FG as the first Eighth Air Force's fighter group to commence combat operations. The unit, however, was transferred on 14 September 1942 to the Twelfth Air Force for operations in North Africa and flew its last mission with the Eighth Air Force on 9 October 1942. The code letters MX, HL and WQ – later reassigned within the Eighth Air Force to the 82nd, 83rd and 84th Fighter Squadrons of the 78th FG – were borne by Spitfires of the group's 307th, 308th and 309th Fighter Squadrons.

16. The only Eighth Air Force unit to fly Thunderbolts throughout its assignment in the ETO was the 56th FG. The famous 56th FG began combat operations on 13 April 1943 and destroyed more enemy aircraft in air combat (674.5 aircraft) than any other USAAF unit. Illustrated is a P-47D-2-RE (42-8369) with squadron code (61st FS) and individual aircraft letter applied with stencil. (Robert Baseler)

flew its first combat mission on 28 December, 1943. From that time until July 1944 the unit flew P-38Hs and P-38Js until re-equipped with Mustangs. Its

17. Capt. Gerald E. Budd's P-47D-22-RE (42-25871) 'Roger the Lodger' at the Eighth Air Force's Station F-357, Duxford on 16 September 1944. The aircraft bears the black-and-white checkerboard cowling of the 78th FG, and the code (WZ) of the 84th Fighter Squadron. (USAF)

Single-seat fighters of the Eighth and Ninth Air Forces
Comparative strength by type (in group-months *)
1942–1945

		Eighth Air Force		Ninth Air Force		Eighth & Ninth Air Forces	
Spitfire	Group-months	10		—		10	
	% of total		3·2		—		1·8
P-38	Group-months	28		32		60	
	% of total		9·0		12·8		10·7
P-47	Group-months	109		192		301	
	% of total		35·2		76·8		53·8
P-51	Group-months	163		26		189	
	% of total		52·6		10·4		33·7
TOTAL	Group-months	310		250		560	
	% of total		100·0		100·0		100·0

*For the purpose of this analysis, a group-month is defined as one group of fighters on operations for one month; thus, ten group-months could represent either one group of fighters on operations for ten months, or ten groups of fighters on operations for one month, or any equal combination of groups and months of operations.

52nd FIGHTER GROUP

Like the 31st FG, the 52nd FG had been scheduled to fly P-39Fs across the Atlantic but was equipped with Spitfire Vbs following its transfer to England in July 1942. The group was transferred to the Twelfth Air Force on 14 September 1942 and only a few sorties were flown in August and September 1942 by its 2nd and 4th Fighter Squadrons whilst the 52nd FG was assigned to the Eighth Air Force.

55th FIGHTER GROUP

Perhaps the best-known unit to fly Lightnings in the ETO, the 55th FG had been activated at Hamilton Field, California, on 15 January 1941 and moved to Nuthampstead, Herts., in September 1943. Flying P-38Hs, the group began combat operations on 15 October 1943 and obtained P-38Js in December of that year. However, in July 1944, three months after moving to Wormingford, Essex, the 55th FG was re-equipped with Mustangs. Thus, it was whilst flying P-51s that the group earned two DUCs for missions between 3 and 13 September 1944, when it claimed the destruction of 106 enemy aircraft, and for ground strafing operations on 19 February 1945. Lt. Col. Elwyn Righetti, the group's Executive Officer, became the Eighth Air Force's top strafing ace with 27 enemy aircraft destroyed (plus 7.5 in the air) but he was killed by civilians following a crash landing after strafing an airfield near Dresden on 17 April 1945. The Lightnings and Mustangs of its 38th, 338th and 343rd Fighter Squadrons bore the code letters, CG, CL and CY, respectively.

56th FIGHTER GROUP

Foremost exponent of the Thunderbolt, this group destroyed more enemy aircraft in the air (674.5 plus 311 on the ground) than any other Eighth Air Force unit. Trained on P-39s and P-40s following its activation at Savannah, Georgia, on 15 January 1941, the 56th FG became in June 1942 the first USAAF unit to receive P-47Bs. By the time it arrived in England, the 56th FG had been re-equipped with combat-worthy P-47Cs and went into operations on 13 April 1943 from Horsham St Faith, Norfolk. Three months later the unit moved to Halesworth, Suffolk, from where it operated when it earned its first DUC for air combats between 20 February and 9 March 1944. Soon thereafter, the 56th FG moved to Boxted, Essex, where it remained until after VE-

18. Carrying a 500 lb bomb on its belly rack, a P-47D-6-RE (42-74676) of a Ninth Air Force squadron takes off from an airstrip in France on a ground-support mission. (USAF)

Day. Even though all the other fourteen fighter groups of the Eighth Air Force exchanged their Lightnings and Thunderbolts, this group remained faithful to the Republic fighter and became the only USAAF unit to fly P-47Ms, which it flew until the

19. P-47D-28-REs of a unit attached to the First Tactical Air Force (Provisional) taxy on the pierced-steel planking of an advanced air base in France. High-explosive bombs are carried beneath the wings whilst anti-personnel bombs are on the centreline rack. (USAF)

end of the war. The code letters HV, LM and UN – first assigned by the Eighth Air Force to the squadrons of the 1st FG – were used on the aircraft of its 61st, 62nd and 63rd Fighter Squadrons.

The 56th FG pilots included six of the ten top-scoring aces (the 1st, 3rd, 5th, 7th, 9th and 10th) of the Eighth Air Force – Lt. Col. Francis Gabreski (28 air victories), Maj. Robert Johnson (27 victories), Lt. Col. David Schilling (22.5 victories), 1st Lt. Fred Christensen (21.5 victories), Maj. Walker Mahurin (20.75 victories) and Col. Hubert Zemke (17.75 victories). Though assigned to the Eighth Air Force and flying primarily bomber escort missions, the 56th FG won its second DUC on 18 September 1944 for support of airborne forces at Arnhem.

78th FIGHTER GROUP

This fighter group shared with the 56th the distinction of having the longest combat record of the fighter groups originally assigned to the Eighth Air Force (the 4th FG had a longer record but, technically speaking, was not assigned to the Eighth Air Force, but rather formed within it). The 78th FG had been activated at Baer Field, Indiana on 9 May 1942 and had trained on Lightnings at Hamilton Field, California before moving to Goxhill, Yorks., for operational training in the ETO. The 78th FG exchanged its P-38Gs for P-47Cs prior to commenc-

ing operations from Duxford, Cambs. on 13 April 1943 where it remained until the end of the war. The group was re-equipped with P-47Ds in June 1943 and with P-51Ds and P-51Ks at the end of 1944.

The 78th FG was unique among Eighth Air Force groups because it won its two DUCs for operations other than bomber escort. The first DUC was earned for supporting airborne forces in Holland between 16 and 23 September 1944, and the second was won on 16 April 1945 when the group destroyed 125 enemy aircraft on the ground – the Eighth Air Force's record claim for a day – when attacking an airfield in the Prague–Pilsen area. MX, HL and WZ were the code letters assigned to the group's 82nd, 83rd and 84th Fighter Squadrons.

339th FIGHTER GROUP

Penultimate fighter group to be assigned to the Eighth Air Force, the unit had been activated at Hunter Field, Georgia on 10 August 1942 as the 339th Bombardment Group (Dive), but the unit's role was changed to fighting before its assignment to the ETO. The 339th FG began combat operations on 30 April 1944 whilst flying Mustangs from Fowlmere, Cambs. Its P-51s bore the codes D7, 5Q and 6N, identifying respectively the 503rd, 504th and 505th Fighter Squadrons. The 339th FG won a DUC for escort missions on 10 and 11 September 1944 when it claimed the destruction of 58 enemy aircraft.

352nd FIGHTER GROUP

Activated on 1 October 1942 and trained in Massachusetts, Connecticut, and New York states, the 352nd FG and its three P-47-equipped squadrons, the 328th, 486th and 487th FS (code PE, PZ and HO) moved to England in June/July 1943. Based at the Eighth Air Force Station 141 at Bodney, Norfolk, the group flew its first combat mission on 9 September 1943 whilst equipped with razorback P-47Ds. It converted to North American P-51Bs during April 1944 and subsequently received P-51Cs, P-51Ds and P-51Ks. The 352nd FG was one of the few Eighth Air Force fighter units to be based on the Continent; it operated from Asche and Chièvres, Belgium, from late December 1944 (group detailed to the Ninth Air Force from 23 December 1944 to 31 January 1945) until 13 April 1945 when the unit moved back to Bodney. It flew its last mission on 3 May 1945.

20. Lying on the port wing of a Thunderbolt of the 10th Fighter Squadron, 50th FG, First Tactical Air Force (Provisional), a crew chief assists the pilot in taxying on a snow-covered airfield in northern France. This photograph was taken at the time when Thunderbolts and their pilots distinguished themselves by helping to halt the German offensive in the Ardennes. (USAF)

During its service with the Eighth Air Force, the group received DUCs for escorting bombers to Brunswick, West Germany, on 8 May 1944 (487th FS only), and for destroying 23 enemy aircraft on 1 January 1945. The group's top-scoring ace was George E. Preddy who was credited with 25 air-to-air kills, 4 shared air victories, and 5 aircraft on the ground, whilst Lt. Col. John C. Meyer, the group's executive officer, shot down 24 aircraft and destroyed 13 on the ground.

353rd FIGHTER GROUP

Pioneer of dive-bombing and ground-attack techniques adopted by P-47 units of the Eighth and Ninth Air Force, the 353rd FG started its combat career on 9 August 1943 whilst stationed at Metfield, Suffolk. It had been activated on 1 October 1942 at Mitchel Field, New York, and had initially been based at Goxhill, Yorks. when it joined the Eighth Air Force in June 1943. The 353rd FG and its 350th, 351st and 352nd Fighter Squadrons (coded LH, YJ and SX) flew Thunderbolts in combat until November 1944 and earned a DUC for support of airborne landings at Nijmegen and Arnhem, Holland, between 17 and 23 September 1944. Less

21. Front view of a Thunderbolt of the 353rd Fighter Group, Eighth Air Force, showing to advantage the devastating punch packed by this type of aircraft for short-range ground-attack sorties: two 1,000 lb bombs, one 500 lb bomb and eight 0·50 machine guns with 425 rpg. (USAF)

22. Typical scene at a USAAF base depot in England with a P-47D-27-RE (42-27249) taxying between a B-17G (foreground) and some P-38Js, a P-47D and an A-20G (background). The Thunderbolts in this photograph carry the red cowling band which identified the 56th FG since March 1944. (USAF)

than two weeks later the group began re-equipping with Mustangs and it flew colourfully marked P-51Ds and P-51Ks until the end of the war.

355th FIGHTER GROUP

Stationed at Steeple Morden, Cambs., the 355th FG flew P-47Ds in combat beginning on 14 September 1943 and Mustangs from March 1944 until the end of the war. Less than one month after converting to P-51Bs, the group earned a DUC for an attack on a German airfield. The 355th FG had been activated on 12 November 1942 at Orlando, Florida, and was composed of the 354th, 357th and 358th Fighter Squadrons (codes WR, OS and YF). With 502.5 enemy aircraft destroyed on the ground, it was the top ground-strafing unit of the Eighth Air Force.

356th FIGHTER GROUP

In 413 missions from 15 October 1943 to VE-Day, the 356th FG destroyed 276.5 enemy aircraft (201 in air combat) but lost 122 aircraft in action, thus earning 'recognition' for being the Eighth Air Force's fighter group with the highest ratio of losses to enemy aircraft claims. It had been activated at Westover Field, Mass., on 12 December 1942 and flew Thunderbolts (until November 1944) and Mustangs from Martlesham Heath, Suffolk. The code letters OC, PI and QI were worn by the aircraft of its 359th, 360th and 361st Fighter Squadrons. The 356th FG won a DUC for support of troops in Holland during October 1944.

357th FIGHTER GROUP

Originally assigned to the Ninth Air Force, the 357th FG was traded at the end of January 1944 for the 358th FG, which had begun combat operations with the Eighth Air Force on 20 December 1943. Thus, the newly created Ninth Air Force gained an experienced P-47 unit whilst the Eighth Air Force obtained its first highly-coveted P-51Bs. Activated at Hamilton Field, California, on 1 December 1942, and trained on Bell P-39s, the group was stationed at Raydon, Suffolk when it was assigned to the Ninth Air Force on 30 November 1943. Upon being transferred to the Eighth AF, the unit replaced the 358th FG at Leiston, Suffolk, from where it started

23. P-47C-2-RE (41-6214) of the 335th Fighter Squadron, 4th FG, Eighth Air Force carrying a 108 US gallon paper tank beneath the fuselage. Markings are standard for the period (the 4th FG flew Thunderbolts from March 1943 through February 1944) and include white identification bands on the front of the cowling (24in width), around the vertical tail surfaces (12in width) and the tailplanes (15in width), and red-bordered national insignia. (USAF)

combat operations on 11 February 1944. Two DUCs were won by the 357th FG for escort missions on 6 March and 29 June 1944 and on 14 January 1945. Aircraft of the group's component 362nd, 363rd and 364th FSs carried the codes G4, B6 and C5 respectively.

359th FIGHTER GROUP

Stationed at East Wretham, Norfolk, this group flew Thunderbolts in combat from 13 December 1943 until early May 1944 when it was re-equipped with

24. Bombed up P-47D-28-REs of the 353rd Fighter Squadron, 354th FG, Ninth Air Force, taxying in preparation for a tactical sortie. Aircraft from this squadron had their cowling painted yellow. Note anti-glare panel extending fore and aft of the cockpit. (USAF)

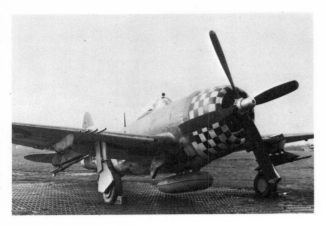

25. Interesting experiment to increase the already formidable armament of the P-47D. This Thunderbolt, the aircraft of Col. Frederic C. Gray, CO of the 78th FG, Eighth Air Force, was fitted with a 20 mm cannon attached to both wing pylons. The photograph was taken at Duxford on 24 October 1944. (USAF)

Mustangs. The 359th FG had been activated at Westover Field, Mass., and was composed of the 368th, 369th and 370th Fighter Squadrons to which the code letters CV, IV and CR/CS were assigned by the Eighth Air Force. The group had a relatively colourless operational career but earned a DUC for successfully protecting the heavy bombers during a raid against Merseburg on 11 September 1944. Maj. Ray Wetmore, the CO of its 370th FS, gained fame for scoring most of its 22 air combat victories during 1945, when encounters with the Luftwaffe were not as frequent as earlier in the war.

26. Second Lt. Alvin Juchheim of the 4th FG with his crew chief, S/Sgt. Robert McCord. The aircraft is a P-47C, the first model of the Thunderbolt to be flown in combat. (USAF)

361st FIGHTER GROUP

Albeit serving in operations from 21 January 1944, the 361st was the only combat fighter unit in the Eighth Air Force not to win a single DUC. Activated on 10 February 1943 at Richmond, Virginia, the group began combat operations from Little Walden, Essex, but was transferred to St Dizier, France at the time of the German offensive in the Ardennes. It operated in France from 25 December 1944 until 15 February 1945 when it moved to Chièvres, Belgium; on 9 April 1945 it returned to its Essex base where it remained until after the end of the war. In the ETO, its 374th, 375th and 376th Fighter Squadrons flew Thunderbolts (December 1943–May 1944) and Mustangs (from mid-May 1944) which bore the codes B7, E2 and E9.

364th FIGHTER GROUP

Activated at Glendale, California on 1 June 1943, this group trained on Lightnings and started combat operations with P-38Js on 3 March 1944. The 364th FG converted to P-51Ds in late July 1944 and, throughout its assignment to the Eighth Air Force, it was based at Honington, Suffolk. The codes N2, 5Y and 5E were used on aircraft of its 383rd, 384th and 385th Fighter Squadrons and the group was unique amongst Eighth Air Force fighter units in painting these codes aft of the national insignia of its Mustangs. The P-51Ds also carried white individual aircraft letters inside the black circle, square and triangle which identified the three squadrons respectively. The group won a DUC for defence of bombers during the 27 December 1944 mission against Frankfurt.

479th FIGHTER GROUP

Last fighter group to join the Eighth Air Force, the 479th shared with the 20th FG the distinction of being the only unit of this air force to win a DUC (for strafing airfields on 18 August and 5 September 1944 and for air combat on 28 September) whilst flying Lightnings. The group had been activated at Glendale, California, on 15 October 1943 and flew P-38Js (first combat mission on 26 May 1944) and P-51Ds (from September 1944 until VE-Day) from Wattisham, Suffolk. Both types of aircraft bore the codes L2, J2 and 9B, which identified the 434th, 435th and 436th Fighter Squadrons. On 25 April 1945 one of the 479th FG pilots, Lt. Hilton Thompson, shot down an Arado Ar234 jet bomber near Salzburg, Austria, to claim the destruction of the last enemy aircraft by the Eighth Air Force.

Ninth Air Force

36th FIGHTER GROUP

Formed on 1 February 1940 as part of the US Army Air Corps prewar expansion programme, the 36th Pursuit Group flew P-39s and P-40s from Puerto Rico until returned to the United States in May/June 1943. After training on Thunderbolts and being redesignated 36th FG, the unit moved to Kingsnorth, England as part of the Ninth Air Force. It was made up of the 22nd, 23rd and 53rd FGs which were coded 3T, 7U and 6V. The first mission of the 36th FG was flown on 8 May 1944 from Kingsnorth, then the unit moved to France, successively operating from bases at Brucheville, Le Mans, Athies and Juvincourt between July and October 1944; to Belgium where it was based at Le Culot from October 1944 through March 1945; and then to Germany, based at Aachen, Niedermendig and Kassel Rothwestern, where it was on VE-Day. As could be expected from a fighter unit assigned a tactical role with the Ninth Air Force, the 36th FG won two DUCs for

27. The use of pierced-steel planking enabled Engineer Aviation Battalions to build advanced air bases in less than two weeks. One of these bases is seen used by P-47D-27-RAs of the 404th Fighter Squadron, 371st FG, First Tactical Air Force (Provisional). (USAF)

Technical Sergeant, US 8th Air Force, 1943. This NCO wears regulation service and walking-out uniform of 'Olive Drab' wool tunic, trousers, shirt and tie, the latter two items of slightly varying shades. The 'overseas cap' of Olive Drab material is piped around the turn-up with Army Air Force colours – orange and ultramarine. On his left lapel appears a round brass badge with the Air Force winged propeller device; on the right is a badge bearing the 'U.S.' cypher. The 8th A.F. patch is worn on the left shoulder, chevrons of this rank on both sleeves, and a three-year service stripe on the left cuff.

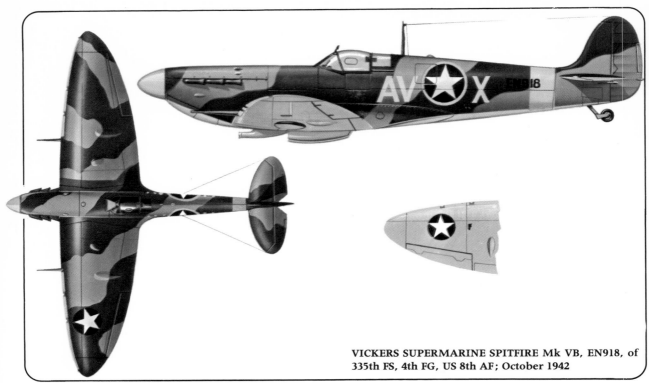

VICKERS SUPERMARINE SPITFIRE Mk VB, EN918, of
335th FS, 4th FG, US 8th AF; October 1942

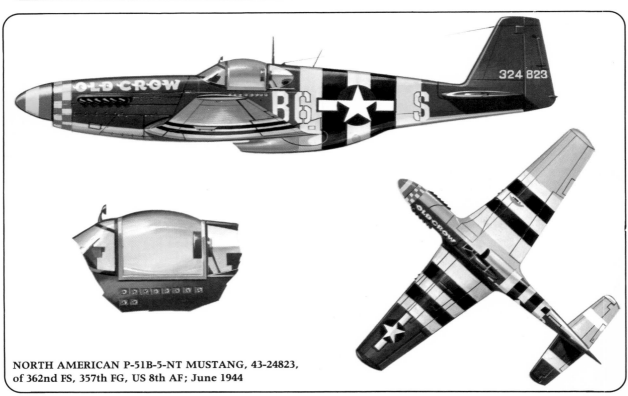

NORTH AMERICAN P-51B-5-NT MUSTANG, 43-24823,
of 362nd FS, 357th FG, US 8th AF; June 1944

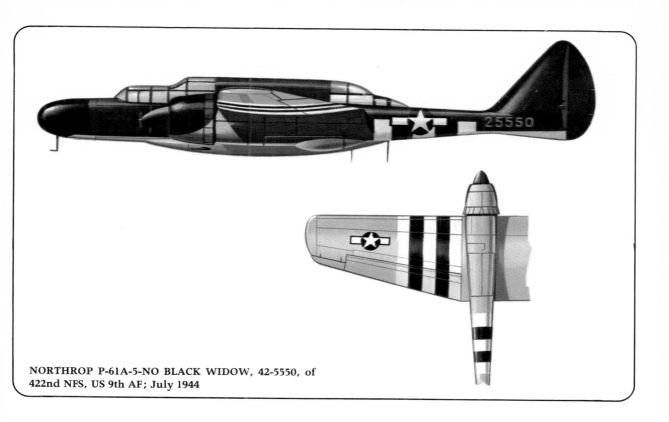

NORTHROP P-61A-5-NO BLACK WIDOW, 42-5550, of
422nd NFS, US 9th AF; July 1944

OPPOSITE TOP: Vickers Supermarine Spitfire Mk VB,
serial EN918, AV-X, of the 335th Fighter Squadron, 4th
Fighter Group, VIII Fighter Command, US 8th Air
Force, based at Debden, England, in October 1942. This
squadron was re-designated from No. 121 ('Eagle') Sqn,
RAF. The Spitfire carries the normal RAF camouflage of
the period in Dark Green and Ocean Grey shadow
shading on upper and side surfaces, with Medium Sea
Gray under surfaces. The spinner, 18-inch fuselage
band, and the squadron (AV) and individual aircraft
codes (X) are all in Sky Type S. Note 4-inch yellow
stripes along wing leading edges. The national insignia
above and below starboard wings are in the form of
white stars on 32-inch blue discs; on the fuselage sides
the 32-inch discs have an additional 2-inch yellow
surround. Codes appear as X-AV on starboard side.

OPPOSITE, BOTTOM: North American P-51B-5-NT Mustang, 43-24823, of the 362nd Fighter Squadron, 357th
Fighter Group, 66th Fighter Wing, VIII Fighter Command, US 8th Air Force. 'Old Crow' was flown by
Captain Clarence E. Anderson from Leiston, England,
in June 1944. Finished in standard Olive Drab/Neutral
Gray scheme, this Mustang had temporary 18-inch

black and white 'invasion stripes' round the wings and
rear fuselage, and the red and yellow recognition
scheme of the 357th Fighter Group on the spinner and
nose. Squadron (B6) and individual aircraft codes (S)
appear in white on both sides of the fuselage, outlined
black where they fall on white invasion stripes. The 15-
inch white recognition bands round each side of the
tailplane are a relic of the wing and tail stripe system
adopted earlier to prevent confusion between Mustangs and Bf109s in the haste of air combat. Note the
bare metal framing of the sliding cockpit hood, and
details of Anderson's 'kill' markings. Note that plan
view is split upper/lower presentation.

ABOVE: Northrop P-61A-5-NO Black Widow, 42-5550 of
the 422nd Night Fighter Squadron, U.S. 9th Air Force,
based at Mauperthuis, France in July 1944. As normal
for night fighters, this Black Widow is finished in a
dull scheme: Olive Drab and Neutral Gray, with matt
Insignia Red serials on the tail booms. The effect is
largely destroyed by the marking of 'invasion stripes'
on the lower and side surfaces and the carrying of the
normal national insignia, however small. The flat black
area on the nose is the radome.

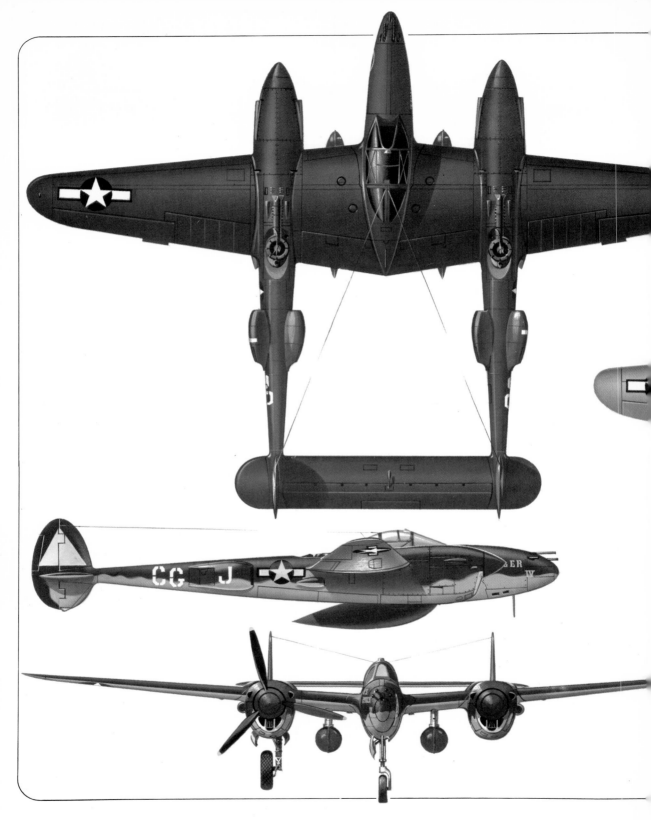

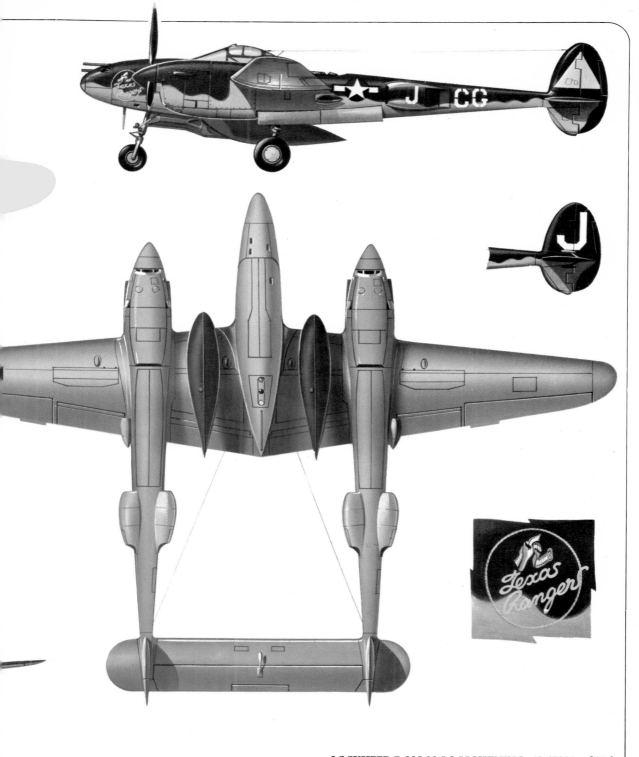

LOCKHEED P-38J-10-LO LIGHTNING, 42-67825, of 38th FS, 55th FG, US 8th AF; March 1944

PAGES 28–29: Lockheed P-38J-10-LO Lightning, 42-67825, 'Texas Ranger IV', in which Col. Jack S. Jenkins, CO of the 55th Fighter Group, 66th Fighter Wing, VIII Fighter Command, US 8th Air Force, led the first Allied fighter formation to reach Berlin on 3 March 1944. Bearing the codes (CG) of the 38th Fighter Squadron, this aircraft was based at Nuthampstead, England in March 1944. The standard Olive Drab/Neutral Gray scheme is displayed, with natural metal undercarriage legs, wheel hubs, and engine intake lips. Note differing presentations of aircraft name on port and starboard nose sides: colour of lettering appears from a wartime colour photograph to be either a faded and yellowed Insignia White, or a deliberately mixed buff shade. A detail view illustrates the individual aircraft letter (J) painted on the inside surface of each tail fin. The national insignia on the fuselage booms are based on a 20-inch diameter disc, and those on the wings on a 30-inch diameter disc. Drop tanks are Olive Drab, and the inside of the undercarriage door is painted in Zinc Chromate, a yellowish light green.

Aircraft modellers might care to note that the wartime colour photograph mentioned above shows Col. Jenkins in flying clothing comprising a dark brown leather helmet with his surname across the brow in white block letters; British Army Khaki battledress blouse with 8th Air Force patch on the left shoulder; white scarf; standard yellow life-jacket; and pale khaki drill 'chino' trousers.

BELOW: Republic P-47D-28-RA Thunderbolt, 42-28929, of 405th Fighter Squadron, 371st Fighter Group, XIX Tactical Air Command, US 9th Air Force, based at Metz-Frescaty, France, in March 1945. In natural metal finish, this Thunderbolt has Insignia Blue identification markings on cowling and tail fin, and Insignia Red on the rudder. Note Olive Drab anti-glare panel continued behind the cockpit, passing right down each side of the fuselage strake which was added to late-model bubble-canopy P-47Ds to improve control. The codes 8N identify the squadron, and X (note unusual pre-sentation, due to position partly below tailplane) the individual aircraft. The centre-line strongpoint carries a 500-lb bomb, and each wing strongpoint a 1,000-lb bomb; all are painted Olive Drab. Note extra large (40-inch diameter disc) wing insignia, and 35-inch diameter disc fuselage insignia. It was for ground-attack missions between 15 and 21 March 1945 that this group was awarded a Distinguished Unit Citation.

OPPOSITE, TOP: Selection of Fighter Group identification markings, US 8th Air Force: (A)=55th FG, from July 1944. (A1)=343rd FS, code CY; (A2)=338th FS, code CL; (A3)=38th FS, code CG. (B)=78th FG, from December 1944. (B1)=84th FS, code WZ; (B2)=83rd FS, code HL; (B3)=82nd FS, code MX. (C)=56th FG, from May 1944. (C1)=63rd FS, code UN; (C2)=62nd FS, code LM; (C3)=61st FS, code HV. (D)=20th FG, from July 1944. (D1)=55th FS, code KI; (D2)=79th FS, code MC; (D3)=77th FS, code LC.

OPPOSITE, BOTTOM: Willys $\frac{1}{4}$-ton 4×4 General Purpose field car – the ubiquitous 'jeep', used in huge quantities by every US military organization and the standard runabout on and around US Army Air Force bases the world over. This example has a couple of non-regulation markings typical of the 8th Air Force's jeeps.

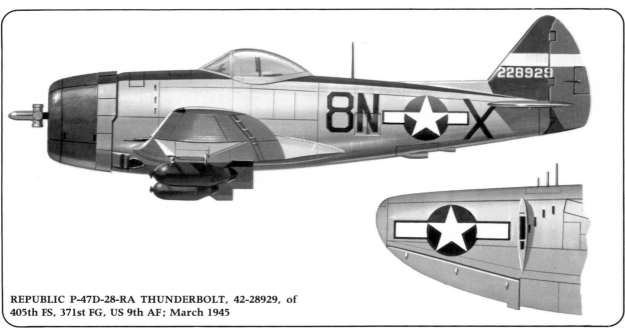

REPUBLIC P-47D-28-RA THUNDERBOLT, 42-28929, of 405th FS, 371st FG, US 9th AF; March 1945

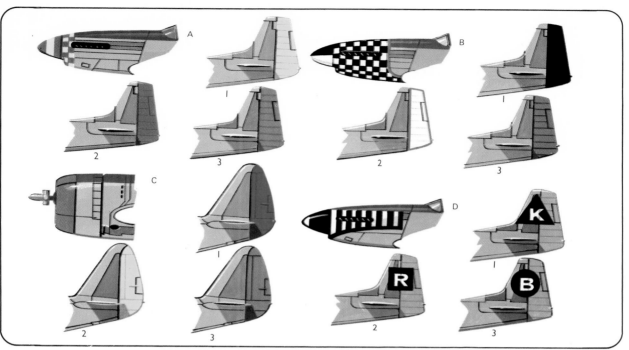

A

1

2

3

B

1

2

3

C

1

2

D

K

R

B

1

2

3

WILLYS ¼-ton 4 × 4 General Purpose truck – 'Jeep'

BELOW: Fighter pilot, 8th Air Force, 1943–44. He wears one of several patterns of leather flying helmet with single-lens goggles pushed up and radio jack-plug hanging. The life-jacket is regulation issue; the boots appear to have been acquired from RAF stock. The flying jacket and trousers are of a slightly sateen-finish Olive Drab fabric, with knitted woollen wrist and waistbands; the jacket has a collar faced with a short brown pile. The 8th Air Force patch is worn on the left shoulder only.

ABOVE: Mechanic, 8th Air Force, 1943–44. Huddled against the East Anglian winter wind – rumoured to come straight from the Urals – this groundcrew soldier wears the regulation Olive Drab fatigue cap and one-piece overalls. His rubber storm-boots are closed by four metal straps. Like most groundcrew, he has acquired a fleece-lined flying jacket of aircrew issue – similar to the British Irvin jacket, but less heavily constructed and with a lighter lining of white fleece.

strafing/bombing missions: one a ground-attack operation on 1 September 1944 when the unit disrupted the German retreat south of the Loire, and the other an attack against airfields in southern Germany on 12 April 1945.

48th FIGHTER GROUP

Also flying Thunderbolts throughout its thirteen months of combat operations with the Ninth Air Force, this unit had been activated at Savannah, Georgia on 15 January 1941 as the 48th Bombardment Group (Light). Exchanging its twin-engined Douglas A-20s and B-18s for single-engined A-24s, A-31s, A-35s, A-36s, P-34s and P-40s, this unit was redesignated the 48th Bombardment Group (Dive) in September 1942 but remained in the United States until March 1944. Finally redesignated 48th Fighter Group and equipped with P-47s, it was assigned to the Ninth Air Force in March 1944 and was based at Ibsley, England at the time of its combat debut on 20 April 1944. Following the landing in Normandy, the 48th FG moved in July 1944 to France (Deaeux Jumeaux, Villacoublay and Cambrai/Niergnies); in September 1944 to St Trond, Belgium; and in March 1945 to Germany (Kelz, Kassel and Illesheim). It received a single DUC for effective ground-support operations on 6 December 1944 in spite of heavy overcast and intense flak opposition. Components of the 48th FG were the 492nd (F4), 493rd (I7) and 494th (6M) Fighter Squadrons.

50th FIGHTER GROUP

Designated 50th Pursuit Group when activated at Selfridge Field, Michigan, on 15 January 1941, the unit served with the AAF Fighter Command School and AAF School of Applied Tactics in Florida before March 1944, when it was assigned to the Ninth Air Force as a Thunderbolt fighter group. First stationed in England at Lymington, Hants – from where the first combat mission was flown on 1 May 1944 – the 50th FG then followed the American troops on the Continent, being stationed in France at Carentan (from 25 June 1944, less than three weeks after D-Day), Meautis, Orly, Laon, Lyon/Bron, and Toul/Ochey; and in Germany at Giebelstadt and Mannheim. The components of the 50th FG were

28. 'Chunky', a razorback Thunderbolt of the 358th FG with a mixed load of two 1,000 lb bombs and one drop tank. The four-blade propeller being turned by mechanics is a 12 ft 2 in Curtiss Electric unit driven by a 2,000/2,300 hp Pratt & Whitney R-2800-63 engine. (USAF)

the 10th, 81st and 313th Fighter Squadrons, coded T5, 2N and W3. Collectively, they won a DUC in March 1945 for close co-operation with the Seventh Army during the assault on the Siegfried Line, and a second DUC for an airfield attack on 25 April 1945. From 29 September 1944 through 31 October, control of the 50th FG was temporarily transferred to the XII Tactical Air Command, Twelfth Air Force,

29. P-47D-22-REs (42-25904, 2N-U 'Lethal Liz II' in foreground) of the 81st Fighter Squadron 50th FG, Ninth Air Force, sharing a pastoral Normandy setting with some obviously undisturbed cows. A Fleet Air Arm Seafire III from one of the four FAA squadrons assigned to No. 34 (P.R.) Wing, RAF, as part of the Air Spotting Pool appears in the distance, with collapsed undercarriage. (USAF)

FIGHTER GROUPS AND THEIR AIRCRAFT, 9TH AIR FORCE, 1943–45

Key: (+) P-38; (=) P-47; (*) P-51

Unit	1943		1944												1945				
	N	D	J	F	M	A	M	J	J	A	S	O	N	D	J	F	M	A	M
36th FG							=	=	=	=	=	=	=	=	=	=	=	=	=
48th FG						=	=	=	=	=	=	=	=	=	=	=	=	=	=
50th FG							=	=	=	=	=	to 12th AF (Oct.) & 1st TAF(P) (Nov.) with P-47 throughout							
354th FG		*	*	*	*	*	*	*	*	*	*	*	=	=	=	*	*	*	*
358th FG				=	=	=	=	=	=	=	=	=	=	to 1st TAF(P) with P-47 throughout					
362nd FG				=	=	=	=	=	=	=	=	=	=	=	=	=	=	=	=
363rd FG				*	*	*	*	*	*	*	re-designated 363rd Tac. Recce. Group								
365th FG				=	=	=	=	=	=	=	=	=	=	=	=	=	=	=	=
366th FG					=	=	=	=	=	=	=	=	=	=	=	=	=	=	=
367th FG							+	+	+	+	+	+	+	+	+	=	=	=	=
368th FG					=	=	=	=	=	=	=	=	=	=	=	=	=	=	=
370th FG							+	+	+	+	+	+	+	+	+	*	*	*	*
371st FG						=	=	=	=	=	=	=	to 12th AF & 1st TAF(P)		=	=	=	=	=
373rd FG						=	=	=	=	=	=	=	=	=	=	=	=	=	=
404th FG							=	=	=	=	=	=	=	=	=	=	=	=	=
405th FG						=	=	=	=	=	=	=	=	=	=	=	=	=	=
406th FG						=	=	=	=	=	=	=	=	=	=	=	=	=	=
474th FG						+	+	+	+	+	+	+	+	+	+	+	+	+	+
P-38 groups	0	0	0	0	0	1	3	3	3	3	3	3	3	3	3	1	1	1	1
P-47 groups	0	0	0	3	5	8	13	13	13	13	11	11	14	14	14	14	14	14	14
P-51 groups	0	1	1	2	2	2	2	2	2	2	2	1	1	0	0	2	2	2	2
Total no. of groups	0	1	1	5	7	11	18	18	18	18	15	15	17	17	17	17	17	17	17

30. Yellow-nosed P-51D-5-NA (44-13926, E2-S) of the 375th Fighter Squadron, 361st FG, 67th Fighter Wing, VIII Fighter Command, Eighth Air Force. Note closely grouped muzzles of the three 0·50 in machine guns in the port wing. (USAF)

but effective on 1 November 1944, the group was permanently re-assigned to the 1st Tactical Air Force (Provisional) in support of ground operations by the French 1st Army.

354th FIGHTER GROUP

Proudly named the 'Pioneer Mustang Group', the 354th FG flew its first mission on 1 December 1943 when it introduced the superb P-51B to the ETO. The group had been activated on 15 November 1942 at Hamilton Field, California, and trained in the United States with Bell P-39s. During October and November 1943 the 354th was moved to England to become the first fighter group assigned to the newly created Ninth Air Force. However, as its Mustangs were ideally suited to long-range bomber escort, the unit flew many missions in support of Eighth Air Force operations while still attached to the Ninth Air Force.

The three squadrons constituting 354th FG were 353rd, 355th and 356th FSs, coded FT, GQ and AJ; they were first stationed in England at Boxted, Suffolk and Lashenden, Kent, but, on 23 June 1944, they moved to France and operated successively from Criqueville, Gael, Orconte and Meurthe-et-Moselle until April 1945 when they arrived in Germany (Ober Olm and Ansbach). Maj. James H. Howard of the 356th FS won the Congressional Medal of Honor for single-handedly defending a bomber formation during an escort mission on 11 January 1944. Other honours won by the 'Pioneer Mustang Group' were two DUCs for developing long-range escort missions up to May 1944 and for fighter sweeps on 25 August 1944.

358th FIGHTER GROUP

As the P-51B was better suited to the long-range escort role than was the P-47D, the Eighth and Ninth Air Forces traded the Mustang-equipped 357th FG for the Thunderbolt-equipped 358th. Thus, though it had originally been assigned to the Eighth Air Force, the 358th FG began operations on 3 February 1944 as the Ninth Air Force's second tactical fighter unit. The 348th FG, composed of the 365th (code CH), 366th (IA) and 367th (CP) Fighter Squadrons, had been activated on 1 January 1943 at Richmond, Virginia and had flown its first combat mission from Leiston, Suffolk on 20 December 1943 as an Eighth Air Force unit. Upon being reassigned to the Ninth Air Force, the unit moved to Raydon, Suffolk and then to High Halden, Kent. Beginning in early July 1944, the 358th FG was based on the Continent, first in France (Cretteville, Pontorson, Vitry-le-Francois, Mourmelon and Toul) and finally at Sandhofen, Germany. On 15 November 1944 the 358th FG was permanently transferred to the 1st Tactical Air Force (Provisional). Equipped with Thunderbolts throughout its wartime service, the 358th FG won three DUCs, a record for ETO fighter units, for actions between 24 December 1944 and 2 January 1945, 19 and 20 March 1945, and 8 through 25 April 1945.

31. 'Sky Bouncer', a P-51D-5-NA (44-13568) of the 375th Fighter Squadron, 361st FG, photographed during a practice mission with the 91st Bombardment Group on 20 July 1944. (USAF)

362nd FIGHTER GROUP

Comprising the 377th, 378th and 379th Fighter Squadrons, which respectively used the codes E4, G8 and B8 on their aircraft, the 362nd FG was activated at Westover Field, Massachusetts, on 1 March 1943. After training in P-47s in the northeast United States, the group was assigned to the Ninth Air Force and moved to England during November 1943 to take up its station at Wormingford. The first mission of the 362nd FG was flown on 8 February 1944 from this base, but a change in

32. This inflight plan view of a 375th Fighter Squadron, 361st FG Mustang shows to advantage the beautiful lines of the aircraft, its ventral radiator and the high visibility of the black and white invasion stripes. (USAF)

33. Photographed at Fowlmere on 2 March 1945, this P-51C-10-DT (43-25050) is fitted with a Malcolm hood and carries the red rudder and code (D7) of the 503rd Fighter Squadron, 339th FG, Eighth Air Force. The group markings consisted of a red-white-red ringed spinner and a two-row checkerboard in red and white around the forward 12 inches of cowling. (USAF)

station to Headcorn took place in mid-April 1944. In common with other Ninth Air Force groups, the unit moved to France shortly after D-Day and was successively based at Lignerolles, Rennes, Prosnes and Rouvres before occupying three bases in Germany, Frankfurt, Furth and Illesheim, during the last four weeks of the war.

During its fifteen-month tour of combat duty in the ETO, the 362nd FG won two DUCs for attacks against naval targets in Brest on 25 August 1944 and for armed reconnaissance sorties in support of ground forces operating in the Moselle–Rhine triangle on 16 March 1945.

34. Lt. Col. Roy A. Webb, CO of the 374th Fighter Squadron, 361st FG, in his P-51D-5-NA (44-13626). The aircraft is carrying a drop tank beneath each wing. (USAF)

363rd FIGHTER GROUP

Trained on Bell P-39s, after being activated at Hamilton Field, California on 1 March 1943, the 363rd FG moved to England, without aircraft, to join the Ninth Air Force and received Mustangs at Rivenhall during January 1944. On the 23rd of the following month the group flew its first combat mission and, in April 1944, it moved to Staplehurst. Following D-Day, the 363rd FG was based at Mauperthuis and then Azeville in France but, on 4 September 1944 its mission changed to reconnaissance and it was redesignated 363rd Tactical Reconnaissance Group. While designated 363rd Fighter Group and operating in the Ninth Air Force, the unit had been equipped solely with Mustangs and was made up of the 380th, 381st and 382nd Fighter Squadrons, respectively coded A9, B3 and C3.

365th FIGHTER GROUP

Yet another T-bolt unit, the 365th FG joined the Ninth Air Force in England only six months after having been activated on 15 May 1943 at Richmond Army Air Base, Virginia. Combat operations from Gosfield started on 22 February 1944 but the group moved to Beaulieu, Hants, a few days later. Following advancing American troops on the Continent, the unit was stationed in France at Azeville, Lignerolles, Bretigny and Juvincourt; in Belgium at Chièvres between 28 June 1944 and 26 December 1944. However, as a result of the German advance in the Ardennes, the 365th FG had to move back to Metz, France for a month before resuming its forward moves, which took it successively to Florennes/Juzaine, Belgium, and Aachen and Fritzlar, Germany. Aircraft from its 386th, 387th and 388th Fighter Squadrons bore respectively the codes D5, B4 and C4. The 365th FG won its first DUC on 21 October 1944 for air combat over the Bonn–Düsseldorf area and its second DUC on 29 April 1945 for attacks on airfields, ground transports and ammunition dumps.

366th FIGHTER GROUP

This group was activated at Richmond, Virginia on 1 June 1943, and flew its first combat mission on 14

March 1944 from Thruxton, England. It won a DUC on 11 July 1944 for severely damaging a German tank column in the St Lo area, despite driving rain and intense anti-aircraft fire. Its 389th, 390th and 391st Fighter Squadrons, with Thunderbolts coded A6, B2 and A8, moved to St Pierre du Mont only two weeks after the landings in Normandy. Later, they operated from Dreux/Vermouillet and Laon/Couvron in France, Asche in Belgium, and Munster/Handorf in Germany.

35. SX-I 'Dallas Doll', a P-51D-10-NA (44-14495) of the 352nd Fighter Squadron, 353rd FG, taken at Raydon in December 1944. (USAF)

367th FIGHTER GROUP

Equipped with Bell P-39s after its activation at Hamilton Field, California on 15 July 1943, the 367th FG entered combat operations on 9 May 1944 equipped with Lockheed P-38s and ended the war flying P-47s. Stationed in England at Stony Cross and Ibsley, between April and July 1944, the group then took its Lightnings to Criqueville, Peray, Clastres and Juvincourt in France. It was re-equipped with P-47Ds in February 1945 whilst based at St Dizier, and moved to Conflans prior to leaving France for Frankfurt/Eschborn in Germany on 10 April 1945. DUCs were won by the 367th FG for two fighter sweeps against airfields and trains on 25 August 1944 and for bombing and strafing the headquarters of the German Commander-in-Chief, West, at Ziegenburg on 19 March 1945. The Lightnings and, from February 1945, Thunderbolts flown by the group's 392nd, 393rd and 394th Fighter Squadrons were coded H5, 8L and 4N.

368th FIGHTER GROUP

This group was activated at Westover Field, Massachusetts, on 1 June 1943 and had flown its first combat missions on 4 March 1944. It gained the distinction of being the first USAAF fighter group to operate from an advance air base in newly liberated France when it moved from Chilbolton, England to Cardonville on 19 June 1944 – only 13 days after Allied troops had landed in Normandy. The unit comprised the 395th, 396th and 397th Fighter Squadrons, which were equipped with Thunderbolts until the end of the war, and their aircraft were coded respectively A7, C2 and D3. The 368th FG won a DUC for support operations in the vicinity of

Mons on 3 September 1944 and, following its initial assignment on the Continent at Cardonville, was based successively at Chartres and Laon, France; Chièvres, Belgium; Juvincourt and Metz, France; and Frankfurt-am-Main, Germany.

370th FIGHTER GROUP

Even though it had been trained in P-47s following its activation at Westover Field, Massachusetts, on 1 July 1943, the 370th FG became one of the three Lightning-equipped fighter units of the Ninth Air Force. After arriving in England during February 1944, the group and its three squadrons – the 401st, 402nd and 485th, with aircraft coded 7F, E6 and 9D – became operational at Andover, Hants on 1 May

36. Fitted with the Malcolm hood which substantially improved cockpit visibility and comfort of early Mustangs, this P-51B-5-NA belonged to the 382nd Fighter Squadron, 363rd FG, Ninth Air Force. (USAF)

37. Coded 5E-S and named 'Elsie', this Mustang of the 358th Fighter Squadron, 364th FG, 67th Fighter Wing, 1st Bombardment Division, Eighth Air Force, was photographed on 20 September 1944 at Eighth Air Force Station F-375, Honington, England. (USAF)

38. Assigned to Lt. A. R. Rosatone of the 352nd Fighter Squadron, 353rd FG, this P-51D-15-NA (44-155587) is seen in December 1944 carrying two 108 US gallon drop tanks. At that time, the group marking consisted of black-yellow-black-yellow ringed spinner and three-row checkerboard in black and yellow around the forward 18 inches of cowling. Later, five additional checkerboard rows were added. (USAF)

1944. On 20 July 1944 the 370th FG moved to the Continent and was successively stationed at Cardonville, La Vieille, Lonray and Roye/Amy in France; and Florennes/Juxaine and Zwartzberg in Belgium. Whilst based at Zwartzberg, the group converted to P-51s during February 1945 and operated Mustangs until VE-Day, when operating from Gutersloh, Germany. The 370th FG won a DUC on 2 December 1944 for ground support operations in the Hurtgen Forest area.

371st FIGHTER GROUP

During thirteen months of operations in the ETO, the 371st FG was attached to the Ninth Air Force, then to the Twelfth Air Force, between 29 September and 31 October 1944, then to the 1st Tactical Air Force (Provisional), and, from February 1945 until the end of the war back to the Ninth Air Force. Throughout these changes of command, the group flew Thunderbolts first from Bisterne, England, then from Beuzeville, Perthes, Dole/Tavaux, Tantonville and Metz, France, and Frankfurt/Eschborn, Germany. It had been activated at Richmond, Virginia, on 15 July 1943 and flew its first combat

mission with the Ninth Air Force on 12 April 1944. The only DUC won by the 371st FG and its 404th, 405th and 406th Fighter Squadrons (codes 9Q, 8N and 4W) was for a series of attacks on ground targets between 15 and 21 March 1945 after it had been re-assigned to the Ninth Air Force.

373rd FIGHTER GROUP

This group was composed of the 410th, 411th and 412th Fighter Squadrons, the Thunderbolts of which bore the codes R3, U9 and V5 while they were assigned to the Ninth Air Force. It was activated on 15 August 1943 at Westover Field, Massachusetts, and one month after arriving in England to be based at Woodchurch, the group was operational and flew its first sorties on 8 May 1944 to join other Ninth Air Force units in the intensive pre-D-Day interdiction campaign against airfields, highways and railroads in France. Continuing in this role throughout most of the following twelve months, the 373rd FG was successively stationed at Tour-en-Bassin, St James and Reims, France; Le Culot, Belgium; Venlo, Holland; and Lippstadt, Germany. Whilst operating from Venlo the group played a vital part in supporting the Rhine crossing and won a DUC for a particularly successful mission on 20 March 1945.

39. YJ-M 'Ginny', a P-51D-10-NA of the 351st Fighter Squadron with the extended checkerboard group marking applied to aircraft of the 353rd FG during the winter of 1944–45. The aircraft is seen after running off the runway at Raydon on 23 January 1945. (USAF)

40. Mustang of the 383rd Fighter Squadron, 364th FG, 67th Fighter Wing, Eighth Air Force at Honington on 21 May 1945. Note that the aircraft is fitted with three zero-length launchers for 5in HVAR rockets, a rare load on Eighth Air Force fighters. (USAF)

41. 'Fool's Paradise IV', a P-51D-5-NA of the 380th Fighter Squadron, 363rd FG, Ninth Air Force. Note that upper portions of the invasion stripes have been crudely removed from the fuselage and wings. (USAF)

404th FIGHTER GROUP

Designated 404th Bombardment Group (Dive) when activated at Key Field, Mississippi, this unit was redesignated 404th Fighter-Bomber Group in August 1943 and, finally, 404th Fighter Group when it was assigned to the Ninth Air Force in the spring of 1944. Under this designation, the group flew its first combat mission on 1 May 1944 from Winkton, England before moving to the Continent on 6 July 1944. The 404th FG and its 506th, 507th

42. LH-U 'Don Helen', a Mustang of the 350th Fighter Squadron, 353rd FG landing at Raydon, England. The aircraft has the yellow rudder which denoted the 350th Fighter Squadron from November 1944. (USAF)

and 508th Fighter Squadrons (codes 4K, Y8, and 7J) then flew Thunderbolts from bases in France (La Chapelle, Bretigny and Juvincourt), Belgium (Saint Trond) and Germany (Keltz and Fritzlar). A single DUC was won for three armed reconnaissance missions flown on 10 September 1944 against a variety of targets in Germany.

405th FIGHTER GROUP

The history of the 405th FG closely paralleled that of the 404th, as it was initially activated at Drew Field, Florida, as Bombardment Group (Dive) before being redesignated as Fighter-Bomber Group and finally, upon assignment to the Ninth Air Force, a Fighter Group. Flying Thunderbolts, the 509th, 510th and 511th Fighter Squadrons (codes G9, 2Z and K4) flew their first combat mission on 11 April 1944 from Christchurch, England. Bases on the Continent from which the 405th FG operated beginning on 30 June 1944 were Picauville and St Dizier in France; Ophoven in Belgium; and Kitzingen in Germany. On 24 September 1944, in spite of rain and dense overcast, the group successfully intervened in a major tank battle and hit several other targets as well, to win a DUC.

406th FIGHTER GROUP

Last group of the Ninth Air Force to become operational (on 9 May 1944 from Ashford, England), the 406th FG had also been activated as a Bombardment Group (Dive) at Key Field, Mississippi. After training in the southern United States on a variety of single-engined attack and fighter aircraft, it took its fighter group designation upon being assigned to the ETO during the spring of 1944. Its ground-support activities were rewarded by two DUCs, the second for support of the surrounded ground forces in Bastogne, Belgium, between 23 and 27 December 1944. Equipped with P-47s throughout its service in the ETO, the 406th FG was made up of the 512th, 513th and 514th Fighter Squadrons with aircraft coded L3, 4P and O7.

474th FIGHTER GROUP

This was the only group in the ETO to fly exclusively Lightnings whilst on operations. The

474th FG had been activated at Glendale, California on 1 August 1943. Moving to England in February/March 1944, the group went operational from Moreton on 25 April 1944. Whilst stationed at Neuilly, France, its first base on the Continent, the 474th FG won a DUC on 23 August 1944 for its effective support of ground forces during the breakthrough in the Falaise-Argentan area. It then moved to Saint Marceau and Peronne, France; Florennes, Belgium; and Strassfeld and Langensalza, Germany. The P-38s of its 428th, 429th and 430th Fighter Squadrons were coded 7Y, F5 and K6 and bore a black circle, black square and black triangle, respectively, on the outboard side of their vertical tail surfaces.

SUNDRY FIGHTER-EQUIPPED UNITS OF THE EIGHTH AND NINTH AIR FORCES
In addition to equipping the combat fighter groups, fighters were operated in the ETO as hack, command and monitor aircraft by a number of bomber groups and command units of the USAAF. In addition, the 495th and 496th Fighter Training Groups of the Eighth Air Force flew P-47s, and P-38s and P-51s, respectively, in a non-combat role. The Eighth Air Force also assigned Mustangs to the 1st, 2nd and 3rd Scouting Forces beginning in July 1944, when the 1st Scouting Force was established to provide weather and other relevant information whilst flying a few minutes ahead of the main bomber stream.

Other Ninth Air Force fighter units not previously listed were the 422nd and 425th Night Fighter Squadrons which were equipped with Northrop P-61 Black Widows. These two squadrons were activated at Orlando, Florida, on 1 August and 1 December 1943 respectively, and arrived in England in May 1944. Combat operations began in July 1944 under RAF guidance from English bases but both units moved to the Continent in July and August to provide night cover for American troops, and to fly night interdiction missions. From then until VE-Day the 422nd NFS operated, successively, from two bases in France, one in Belgium and two in Germany. Neither squadron applied code letters or other identification markings to its aircraft.

43. The black rudder and partially obscured code (SX) identifies 'Donna Mite' as being assigned to the 352nd Fighter Squadron of the 353rd FG, Eighth Air Force. The aircraft is a P-51K-5-NT (44-11624). (USAF)

THE AIRCRAFT

Supermarine Spitfire
The Bell P-39 Airacobras and Curtiss P-40 Warhawks—the only types of US fighter aircraft available in large numbers in 1942 — were urgently needed in the Pacific and Mediterranean theatres of operations, and, as they were found by the USAAF to have insufficient performance for the demanding combat environment in Northern Europe, the Eighth Air Force was initially forced to rely on Supermarine Spitfires to supplement the small

44. Flown by Capt. Richard A. Peterson, an ace credited with 15.5 aircraft in the air and 3.5 on the ground, this P-51D-15-NA of the 364th Fighter Squadron, 357th FG, Eighth Air Force, was photographed from the starboard waist position of a flak-damaged Flying Fortress which Capt. Peterson was escorting back to England. (USAF)

AIRCRAFT	Spitfire Vb	P-38F-10-LO	P-38J-15-LO	P-47D-23-RA	P-47M-1-RE	P-51B-1-NA	P-51K-1-NT	P-61A-5-NO
Dimensions:								
Span, ft in	36 10	52 0	52 0	40 9	40 9	37 0	37 0	66 0
(m)	(11·23)	(15·85)	(15·85)	(12·42)	(12·42)	(11·28)	(11·28)	(20·12)
Length, ft in	29 11	37 10	37 10	36 1	36 4	32 3	32 3	48 11
(m)	(9·12)	(11·53)	(11·53)	(11·00)	(11·07)	(9·83)	(9·83)	(14·91)
Height, ft in	9 11	12 10	12 10	14 2	14 9	13 8	13 8	14 8
(m)	(3·02)	(3·91)	(3·91)	(4·32)	(4·50)	(4·17)	(4·17)	(4·47)
Wing area, sq ft	242	328	328	300	300	233	233	664
(sq m)	(22·483)	(30·472)	(30·472)	(27·871)	(27·871)	(21·646)	(21·646)	(61·688)
Weights:								
Empty weight, lb	5,065	12,264	12,780	10,000	10,423	6,985	7,125	20,965
(kg)	(2,297)	(5,563)	(5,797)	(4,536)	(4,728)	(3,168)	(3,232)	(9,510)
Loaded weight, lb	6,750	14,457	15,500	12,500	12,700	8,475	8,600	27,000
(kg)	(3,062)	(6,558)	(7,031)	(5,670)	(5,761)	(3,844)	(3,901)	(12,247)
Maximum weight, lb	—	18,000	21,600	18,300	15,500	11,800	11,600	32,400
(kg)	—	(8,165)	(9,798)	(8,301)	(7,031)	(5,352)	(5,262)	(14,696)
Wing loading, lb/sq ft	27·89	44·08	47·26	41·67	42·33	36·37	36·91	40·66
(kg/sq m)	(136·19)	(215·21)	(230·74)	(203·44)	(206·70)	(177·58)	(180·22)	(198·53)
Power loading, lb/hp	4·59	5·46	5·44	6·25	6·05	6·14	5·77	6·75
(kg/hp)	(2·08)	(2·47)	(2·46)	(2·84)	(2·74)	(2·79)	(2·62)	(3·06)
Performance:								
Maximum speed, mph @ ft	369 @ 19,500	395 @ 25,000	414 @ 25,000	433 @ 30,000	473 @ 32,000	440 @ 30,000	437 @ 25,000	369 @ 20,000
(km/h @ m)	(594 @ 5,945)	(636 @ 7,620)	(666 @ 7,620)	(697 @ 9,145)	(761 @ 9,755)	(708 @ 9,145)	(703 @ 7,620)	(594 @ 6,095)
Cruising speed, mph @ ft	272 @ 5,000	290 @ 10,000	290 @ 10,000	300 @ 10,000	310 @ 10,000	345 @ 25,000	362 @ 25,000	318 @ 25,000
(km/h @ m)	(438 @ 1,525)	(467 @ 3,050)	(467 @ 3,050)	(483 @ 3,050)	(499 @ 3,050)	(555 @ 7,620)	(582 @ 7,620)	(512 @ 7,620)
Climb rate, ft/min	20,000/5·6	20,000/8·8	20,000/7·0	20,000/11·0	32,000/13·4	30,000/12·5	30,000/13·1	20,000/10·3
(m/min)	(6,095/5·6)	(6,095/8·8)	(6,095/7·0)	(6,095/11·0)	(9,755/13·4)	(9,145/12·5)	(9,145/13·1)	(6,095/10·3)
Service ceiling, ft	36,200	39,200	44,000	42,000	41,000	41,800	41,900	33,100
(m)	(11,035)	(11,950)	(13,410)	(12,800)	(12,495)	(12,740)	(12,770)	(10,090)
Normal range, miles	—	425	450	325	650	900	950	400
(km)	—	(685)	(725)	(525)	(1,045)	(1,450)	(1,530)	(645)

–

number of combat-worthy Lockheed P-38Fs it could obtain to equip its fighter groups.

Obtained under reverse lend-lease from RAF stocks, Spitfires used in the fighter role from bases in England by the 4th, 31st and 52nd Fighter Groups were Mk Vbs powered by a 1,470 hp Rolls-Royce Merlin 45 twelve-cylinder Vee liquid-cooled engine driving a three-bladed propeller. They were armed with two 20 mm Hispano cannon and four 0·303 in Browning machine guns. The Spitfire Vb was the fourth major production model of the famous English fighter; it had been preceded in production by the Mk I, which had entered service in August 1938, Mk II and Mk Va, most of which were armed

with eight wing-mounted 0·303in machine guns. Later Spitfire versions were obtained by the USAAF but were not operated by fighter groups in the ETO. Characteristics and performance of the Spitfire Vb are summarized in the table on p. 42.

are summarized in the table on p. 42.

Lockheed P-38 Lightning

The distinctive twin-boomed Lightning traces its origin to a 1936 Army Air Corps circular calling for the development of a twin-engined interceptor capable of exceeding 360 mph (579 kmh) at 20,000 ft (6,095 m). The prototype XP-38, first flown on 27 January 1939, was followed by 9,922 P-38 fighters and F-4 and F-5 photographic reconnaissance aircraft. The initial production models of the Lightning fighter – the YP-38s, P-38s, P-38Ds and P-38Es – were not found acceptable for combat operations and were used exclusively within the United States. Thus, the P-38Fs became the first Lightning version to be used in combat in the ETO by the Eighth Air Force, and one of these aircraft, flown by Lt Elza Shahan of the Iceland-based 27th Fighter Squadron, drew first blood for the aircraft

45. Pilot and radar operator from a night fighter squadron of the Ninth Air Force give a clear idea of the size of the Black Widow, the first US combat-worthy night fighter. Note rear entrance door with built-in ladder in central nacelle. (USAF)

during August 1942. Moreover, P-38Fs were flown in the ETO during an eight-week period in August–October 1942 by the 1st and 14th Fighter Groups prior to their transfer from the Eighth to the Twelfth Air Force. Following the transfer of these two groups to North Africa, no Lightning was flown in combat in the ETO until the debut twelve months later of the P-38H-equipped 55th FG. While the P-38H represented a substantial improvement over earlier Lightning models, it was quickly supplemented by the superior P-38Js and P-38Ls with redesigned engine nacelles. These later versions of the Lightning were flown in combat in the ETO by the 20th, 55th, 364th and 479th FGs of the Eighth Air Force and by the 367th, 370th and 474th FGs of the Ninth Air Force. However, the four Lightning groups of the Eighth Air Force were quickly re-equipped with the superlative North American P-51

Mustang and only the 474th FG of the Ninth Air Force was still flying Lightnings in the ETO on VE-Day.

Standard armament of the P-38Fs, P-38Hs, P-38Js and P-38Ls flown in the ETO consisted of one 20 mm Hispano cannon and four 0·50 in Colt-Browning machine guns mounted in the nose and these aircraft were powered by two Allison V-1710 twelve-cylinder Vee liquid-cooled engines rated at 1,225–1,425 hp on take-off depending on the specific type of power plants used. However, some P-38Js had their nose armament replaced by a glazed nose with extra crew position and Norden bomb sight in order to serve as pathfinders for Lightning fighter bombers. Lightning characteristics and performance details are contained in the table on p. 42.

Republic P-47 Thunderbolt

Introduced into combat in the ETO on 10 March 1943 by pilots of the 4th FG, who were dismayed at the size and weight of their new mount which substantially exceeded that of their nimble and beloved Spitfires, the massive Thunderbolt became the type of fighter aircraft to be most used in the

ETO by USAAF units. Design of the aircraft, which was powered by an eighteen-cylinder Pratt & Whitney R-2800 radial developing between 2,000 and 2,800 hp, had begun in June 1940 to succeed proposals for lighter and smaller aircraft, the XP-47 and XP-47A. First flown on 6 May 1941, the Thunderbolt prototype (XP-47B) was the first of 15,659 fighter aircraft built by Republic, in two factories at Farmingdale (RE) and Evansville (RA), and by Curtiss in St Louis (CU).

Six series of Thunderbolts – the razorback P-47C-RE, P-47D-1-RE/P-47D-22-RE and P-47D-2-RA/P-47D-23-RA, and the P-47D-25-RE/P-47D-30-RE, P-47D-26-RA/P-47D-30-RA, and P-47M-1-RE with cut-down rear fuselage and all-round vision bubble canopy – were flown by 24 fighter groups of the Eighth and Ninth Air Forces. By VE-Day, though supplanted in the fighter escort role by the longer-ranging Mustangs, Thunderbolts still equipped the 56th FG of the Eighth Air Force and constituted the major part of the fighter bomber element of the Ninth Air Force which, in May 1945, had fourteen of its seventeen fighter groups equipped with P-47s.

As an escort fighter, the Thunderbolt initially lacked the range necessary for operating deep into enemy territory. However, development of suitable drop tanks and increased size of internal tanks, beginning with the P-47D-25-REs and -26-RAs, turned the aircraft into a suitable long-range high-altitude aircraft. None the less, the P-47 was

46. Finished glossy black (jet No. 622 in the standard ANA nomenclature) overall and bearing invasion stripes beneath its wings and tail booms, this Ninth Air Force P-61A-5-NO is seen taxying at an advanced air base in France on 27 September 1944. (USAF)

surpassed in this role by the P-51 and the Thunderbolt found a new lease of life in the low-altitude tactical fighter role, for which its ability to survive tremendous battle damages and its exceptionally heavy armament – eight wing-mounted 0·50 in Colt-Browning machine guns and up to 2,500 lb (1,134 kg) of bombs or ten 5 in HVAR rockets – suited it admirably.

North American P-51 Mustang

Unquestionably the best Allied long-range escort fighter – some even argue convincingly that it was the best overall Allied fighter of the war – the Mustang, of which 15,686 were built, almost failed to be developed into one of the all-time great fighter aircraft. Its prototype, the North American NA-73X, was designed and built in 117 days to meet an RAF requirement for a fighter aircraft equal or superior to the Curtiss Kittyhawk I which the British Purchasing Commission had asked North American to build under licence. Powered by an Allison V-1170 twelve-cylinder Vee liquid-cooled engine, the NA-73X was first flown on 26 October 1940 and was followed by 961 similarly-powered Mustang Is, IAs and IIs for the RAF and P-51s, P-51As, A-36As, F-6As and F-6Bs for the USAAF.

In spite of their excellent handling characteristics, these early Allison-powered Mustangs were handicapped by the low-rated altitude of their engine and thus were unsuitable for the type of fighter operations which prevailed in the ETO. Fortunately, following the successful installation by Rolls-Royce of Merlin 61s and 65s on four experimental Mustang Xs, the USAAF recognized the potential of the Merlin-powered Mustang which was placed in production by North American as the P-51B powered by the United States-built Merlin (Packard V-1650-3). But the USAAF had not fully foreseen the potential of the aircraft as a high-altitude escort fighter, and initial assignment of the aircraft was made to the 354th FG of the Ninth Air Force. Initial success of the aircraft in operations in Northern Europe led to a fortunate reversal of this decision and the Eighth Air Force received full priority on delivery of Merlin-powered P-51Bs, P-51Cs, P-51Ds and P-51Ks. Thus, by VE-Day fourteen of the fifteen fighter goups of the Eighth Air Force were equipped with Mustangs while only two fighter groups of the Ninth Air Force had been re-equipped with P-51s.

The Inglewood-built P-51-NA and Dallas-built P-51C-NTs were armed with four wing-mounted 0·50 in Colt-Browning machine guns and they retained the original Mustang canopy (often replaced by a Malcolm hood which provided improved visibility from the cockpit), whereas the P-51D-NAs, P-51D-NTs and P-51K-NTs (the latter differing from the P-51Ds only in the type of propeller fitted) had six wing guns and a cut-down rear fuselage with all-round vision bubble-canopy.

Northrop P-61 Black Widow

The first American aircraft to be designed from the outset as a night fighter, the Black Widow was a large twin-boom, twin-engined aircraft powered by 2,000 hp Pratt & Whitney R-2800 eighteen-cylinder, air-cooled engines. The XP-61 prototype was first flown on 21 May 1942 and, in addition to 13 aircraft built as service test machines, was followed in production by 200 P-61As, 450 P-61Bs and 41 P-61Cs. Design armament for these aircraft, which were fitted with AI radar in the nose of the central nacelle, consisted of four 20 mm cannon in a ventral tray and four 0·50 in machine guns in a remotely-controlled dorsal turret. However, most, if not all, P-61As assigned to the ETO were not fitted with the dorsal turret, as the initial installation of this item resulted in excessive tail-buffeting problems.

Two squadrons of the Ninth Air Force, the 422nd and 425th Night Fighter Squadrons, were the only ETO units to fly P-61s in combat beginning during the summer of 1944.

LÉGENDES

1 Curtiss- P-40C du 33e escadron Chasseurs (33eFS) à bord USS *Wasp* pour transport vers l'Icelande, juillet 1941. 2 P-40C décollant du USS Wasp – notez les points de reconnaissance d'avant-guerre y compris la plaque de l'escadron sur le côté du fuselage. 3 Des pilotes du 309e FS 31e groupe de chasseurs (31e FG) courent vers leurs Spitfires. Le USAAF utilisa les avions de

chasse britanniques jusqu'à qu'il y eut assez de chasseurs modernes de modèle américain disponibles. **4** Le 31e FG commença les opérations avec le Spitfire Vb, le juillet 1942. A l'automne il se déplaça vers l'Afrique du Nord. **5** Trois chasseurs P-38H Lightning du 339e FS à Bassingbourne, décembre 1943. **6 et 7** P-38J Chasseurs Lightning du 38e FS, 55e FG étaient les premiers chasseurs alliés de voler vers Berlin, le 3 mars 1944, grâce à leurs réservoirs d'essence extérieurs de 150 gallons. **8** P-38J, 43-28474, du 434e FS, 479e FG vient atterrir. **9** La version du P-36 avec le nez tombant, un P-38J modifié ou P-38L avec la place de tir du bombardier au nez de l'appareil. **10** Une autre vue du 'nez tombant' Lightning; les lances-bombes pouvaient transporter chacun des poids de 2.000 livres.

11 P-38J 42-68701 du 367e FS, 9e Air Force, après un atterrissage forcé sur le terrain à Poupeville un peu avant l'invasion de Normandie. **12** P-38J du 479e FG 'Riddle's Raiders' se préparant pour une mission de soutien aux bombardiers depuis Wattisham. **13** 'Kokomo' le chasseur personnel P-47D de Maj.-Gen. William E. Kepner, commandant la 2e Division aérienne, 8th Air Force, mars 1945. **14** 'Miss Carriage' un P-47D Thunderbolt photographié le 23 novembre 1944. Notez les insignes nationaux extra-grands sous l'aile, pour identification rapide. **15** Un vieux P-47D repeint avec des points de répères verts et blancs, agissant comme 'Monitor' pour le 491e groupe de Bombardiers. **16** Le 56e FG était le seul unité du 8e Air Force à piloter des Thunderbolts jusqu'à la fin de la guerre; il détruit plus d'appareils ennemis (674.5) que tout autre unité USAAF. Ce P-47D, 42-8369, avait des points de répères de l'escadron du 61e FS. **17** 'Roger the Lodger', le P-47D du Capt. Gerald E. Budd, photographié à Duxford, le 16 septembre 1944. Le capot quadrillé indique le 78e FG, et les lettres WZ, le 84e FS. Numéro de série 42-25871. **18** Les chasseurs de la 9e Force de l'Air décollant d'un terrain français pour une mission de bombardement. **19** Avec des bombes à grande puissance sous les ailes et des bombes anti-personnels sous le fuselage, des Thunderbolts décollent d'une piste faite de plaques d'acier. **20** Un mécanicien du 10e FS. 50e FG couché sur l'aile d'un Thunderbolt et dirigeant le pilote lorsqu'il se déplace à travers un terrain français couvert de neige à l'époque de la Bataille des Ardennes.

21 Thunderbolt de 353e FG expose l'armement massif de ce genre d'avion de chasse: huit ·50 mitrailleurs, deux bombes de 1,000 livres et une bombe de 500 livres. **22** Scène typique d'un dépôt USAAF en Angleterre: P-47Ds (notez la bande rouge autour du capot qui indique le 56e FG) un B-17G, quelques P-38Js et un A-20G. **23** P-47C du 335e FS. 4e FG avec un réservoir d'essence de 108 gallons sous le fuselage. Notez les rayures blanches d'identité et la bordure rouge autour de l'insigne rond national, typique de la fin de 1943. **24** P-47Ds du 353e FG, 354e FG avec capots de moteurs jaunes. Notez les panneaux foncés pour réduire l'éclat du soleil, devant et derrière les carlingues. **25** Equipement expérimental de canons 20mm sous les ailes d'un P-47 du Col. Frederic C. Gray, qui commandait le 78e FG; octobre 1944. **26** Un pilote (2nd Lt. Jucheim) et un mécanicien principal (Staff Sgt. McCord) d'un P-47C du 4e FG. **27** Des pistes en plaques d'acier pourraient être construites en moins de 15 jours. Les appareils ici sont des P-47Ds du 404e FS, 371e FG 1st Tactical Air Force (Provisional). **28** 'Chunky' un Thunderbolt du 358e FG avec deux bombes de 1,000 livres et un réservoir

d'essence extérieur. **29** P-47D Thunderbolts du 81e FS 50e FG 9e Air Force en Normanndie. Le Seafire III démoli en arrière plan fait partie des unités du Fleet Air Arm utilisés pour des missions de reconnaissance photographiques. **30** Un nez haune d'un P-51D (44-13926, E2-S) du 375e FS, 361e FG, 67e Fighter Wing 8e Air Force.

31 'Sky Bouncer' un P-51D Mustang du 375e FS sur un vol d'essai avec le 91e Groupe de Bombardiers en juillet 1944. **32** Les belles lignes de ce P-51D exposé dans cette vue d'en dessous d'un avion du 375e FS. **33** Fowlmere, le 2 mars 1945; P-51C, 43-25050, avec les lettres de code D7 et un gouvernail rouge du 503e FS, 339e FG 8e Air Force. **34** Lt. Col. Roy A. Webb commandant du 374e FS, 361e FG dans son Mustang. **35** 'Dallas Doll', SX-1, 44-14495, un P-51D du 352e FS, 353e FG à Raydon, décembre 1944. **36** Un P-51B du 382e FS, 363e FG avec le dessus de carlingue Malcolm qui améliora considérablement la visibilité. **37** 5E-S 'Elsie 4', un Mustang 358e FS, 364e FG, 67e Fighter Wing, 8th Air Force, Honnington, le 20 septembre 1944 **38** Les points de répères quadrillés noirs et jaunes du 353e FG vus sur l'avion de Lt. Rosatone du 352e FS en décembre 1944; cinq rangs supplémentaires de carrés furent ajoutés plus tard aux points de répères. **39** YJ-M 'Ginny', un P-51D du 351e FS, à Raydon en janvier 1945; notez les points de répères plus grands sur le nez. **40** Mustang de 383e FS, 364e FG à Honnington en mai 1945, c'est rare de voir un 8th Air Force Mustang avec des lances-fusées sous l'aile.

41 'Fool's Paradise IV' un 9th Air Force Mustang du 380e FS 363e FG avec les points de répères de l'invasion D-Day rapidement enlevés de l'aile supérieur et des surfaces du fuselage. **42 et 43** 'Don Helen' a le code LH et le gouvernail jaune du 350e FS 353e FG, 'Donna Mite' a le code SX et le gouvernail noir du groupe de 352e FS. **44** Capt. Richard A. Peterson pilotant son P-51D du 364e FS, 357e FG, Capt. Peterson était un as, on lui attribua 15.5 victoires aériennes. Il fut photographié d'une place de canon d'un B-17 endommagé qu'il ramenait à bon port. **45** Membres de l'equipage d'un escadron de chasseurs de nuit du 9th Air Force posent avec leur P-61 Black Widow. **46** Un P-61 en noir brillant sur un terrain avancé en France, septembre 1944.

Notes sur planches en couleurs

Page 25 : Technical Sergeant, US 8th Air Force en tenue de jour vert-olive, avec une casquette gansée des couleurs de l'Armée de l'Air, orange et blue foncé. Des chevrons de rang sur les deux manches; 8th AF l'écusson sur l'épaule gauche; le galon de trois ans de service sur le poignet gauche.

Page 26 en haut Spitfire Vb EN 918 du 335e FS 4e FG; Debden octobre 1942. Le camouflage réglementaire vert et gris du fuselage et lettres de code en couleur 'Sky Type S'. Les codes AV indiquent l'escadron, et l'X, l'avion individuel. Les insignes nationaux de '32 inch' sur les ailes n'ont pas de cercle extérieur jaune, mais notez ceci sur l'insigne du fuselage. Cet escadron fut repris du No. 121 ('Eagle') escadron RAF. **Page 26 en bas** P-51B, 43-24823 du 362e FS 357e FG; Leiston, juin 1944. 'Old Crow' fut piloté par Capt. Clarence E. Anderson, dont le tableau de victoires aériennes apparaît sous le carlingue; notez la structure en métal non peinte du capot du carlingue. Les points de répères noirs et blancs D-Day sont peints en rayures large de 18 inch et là où les lettres de codes retombent par-dessus les rayures blanches, elles sont soulignées en noir. Les rayures blanches de 15 inch sur l'empennage sont maintenues d'un système antérieur de points de repères qui évita la confusion entre le Mustang et le Bf 109. Les points de repères rouges et jaunes sur le nez sont les insignes du 357e FG.

Page 27 La manque de points de repères sur les surfaces supérieures de ce P-61 Black Widow du 422e Night Fighter Squadron, et le numéro de série en rouge terne doivent être notés. La surface en noir matt du nez est le radome.

Pages 28–29 Dans ce Lockheed P-38J-10-LO, 42-67825, 'Texas Ranger IV', Col. Jack S. Jenkins, commandant du 55e groupe de chasseurs, emmena la première mission de chasseurs à Berlin le 3 mars 1944. Les lettres de code CG sont celles du 38e FS la lettre individuelle de l'avion J apparaît à l'intérieur des deux plans de dérive et le triangle blanc sur l'extérieur des plans de dérive indique le 38e FS. Notez les présentations différentes du nom sur les deux côtés du nez.

Page 30 Republic P-47D, 42-28929, du 405e FS, 371e FG 9th Air Force, basé à Metz-Frescaty, France pour des opérations tactiques mars 1945. L'avion en métal non peint a des points de repères sur le nez et sur l'empennage, des couleurs Insignia Blue et Insignia Red. Notez les panneaux anti-aveuglants 'Olive-Drab' devant et derrière le carlingue; et l'aspect inhabituel de la lettre de code individuelle 'X' de l'avion, à moitié sous l'empennage. Les insignes nationaux sous l'aile tribord sont exceptionnellement grands (un disque de 40 inch de diamètre) pour identification rapide.

Page 31 en haut Les couleurs d'identité des unités de chasseurs du 8th Air Force: A = 55e FG juillet 1944. A1 = 343e FS code CY. A2 = 338e FS code CL. A3 = 38e FS code CG. B = 78e FG, décembre 1944. B1 = 84e FS, code WZ. B2 = 83e FS, code HL. B3 = 82e FS, code MX. C = 56e FG, mai 1944. C1 = 63e FS, code UN. C2 = 62e FS, code LM. C3 = 61e FS, code HV. D = 20e FG, juillet 1944. D1 = 55e FS, code KI. D2 = 79e FS, code MC. D3 = 77e FS, code LC. **Page 31 en bas** Willys ¼ ton 4 × 4 camion tous usages ('Jeep') avec des points de repères typiques: officiels et officieux, d'un groupe de chasseurs du 8th Air Force en Angleterre.

Page 32 à gauche Un mécanicien du 8th Air Force, 1943–44. Il porte une casquette vert-olive et des bleus de travail, avec des bottes d'hiver en caoutchouc attachées avec des pinces en métal et une veste de pilote en peau de mouton chipée à quelque ami d'équipage aérien. La veste américaine resemblait à la veste RAF Irwin, mais moins lourdement fabriquée et avec du molleton blanc.

Page 32 à droit Pilote chasseur, 8th Air Force 1943–44. Il porte un blouson de vol en nylon vert-olive avec un col en molleton marron, et l'insigne à l'épaule du 8th AIr Force. Le casque et gilet de sauvetage sont de distribution réglementaire; les bottes (d'après une photo d'un pilote habillé pareil) apparaissent être de distribution RAF.

ÜBERSCHRIFT

1 Curtiss P-40C des 33. Jagd-Staffel (33.FS) an Bord USS *Wasp* unterwegs nach Island, Juli, 1941. **2** P-40C startet vom USS *Wasp*. Die Markierungen und das Staffelemblem stammen von vorm Krieg. **3** Piloten des 309.FS, 31 Jagd-Gruppe (31.FG) rennen nach ihrer Spitfires. Die USAAF flog diese britische Maschine bis ausreichende moderne amerikanische Jagdflugzeuge vorhanded waren. **4** 31.FG wurden am 26. Juli 1942 rut det Spitfire Vb zum erstenmal eingesetzt. Im Herbst d.J. wurde sie nach Nordafrika versetzt. **5** Drei P-38H Lightning Jagdmaschinen des 338.FS, Bassingbourne, Dezember 1943. **6, 7** P-38J Lightnings des 38.FS, 55.FG waren die ersten allierten Jagdmaschinen die nach Berlin am 3.März 1944 wegen ihrer 150-Gallon (rund 600 Liter) Zusatz-Treibstoffbehälter eingesetzt werden könnten. **8** Eine P-38J, 43-28474, des 434.FS, 479.FG landet. **9** Eine modifizierte P-38J (P-38L) mit Bombenrichterstelle unter der Rumpfspitze angebracht. Sie hien im Soldatenmund 'Schlaffnase'. **10** 'Schlaffnase' – Lightning. Die Bombenbehälter könnten je 2,000 Pfund tragen.

11 P-38J, 42-68701, des 367.FS, 9th Air Force, nach einer Notlandung bei Poupeville kurz nach der Normandie-Landung. **12** P-38J der 479.FG – 'Riddle's Raiders' (Riddles Plünderer) wird für einen Bombenbegleiteinsatz aus Flugplatz Wattisham vorbereitet. **13** 'Kokomo', persönliche P-47D Jagdmaschine Maj. Gen. William E. Kepners, Befehlshaber der 2. Luft-Division, 8th Air Force, März 1945. **14** 'Miss Carriage' (das Misslingen), eine P-47D Thunderbolt. Das Bild wurde am 23. November 1944 gemacht. Die Kokarden an den Flügelunterseiten sind in Übergrosse, der schnellere Erkennungswegen angebracht worden. **15** Veraltete P-47D, grün-weiss anges-trichen, un als 'monitor' für die 491. Bomben-Gruppe eingesetzt zu werden. **16** Die 56.FG war die einzige Gruppe der 8th Air Force die Thunderbolts bis zum Kriegsende flog. Sie vernichte mehr Feindflugzeuge (674.5) als fede andere USAAF Einheit. Diese P-47D, 42-8369, trägt die Staffelmarkierungen des 61.FS. **17** 'Roger the Lodger', P-47D von Capt. Gerald E. Budd, Duxford, 16. September 1944. Die karrierte Motoren-haube bedeutet: 78.FG; die Buchstaben WZ = 84.FS; Flugzeug-nummer – 42-25871. **18** Jagdflugzeuge der 9th Air Force starten von einem Flugplatz in Frankreich für einen Angriff. **19** Diese Thunderbolts, schwer mit Spregstoffbomben unter den Flügeln und Schützenbomben unterm Rumpf beladen, starten von einem mit Stahlplatten überzogenen Flugplatz. **20** Boden-machanikes vom 10.FS, 50.FG. auf dem Flügel einer Thunderbolt liegend, um dem Piloten Richtungsanweisungen zu gebem. Ort: ein Schneebedeckter Flugplatz in Frankreich während der Ardennenschlact.

21 Eine Thunderbolt vom 353.FG zeigt ihre Zähne; acht .50 Zölliger M-Gs, zwei 1,000 lb Bomben und eine 500 lb Bombe. **22** Typische USAAF Depot in England: P-47Ds (rote Motorenhaubestreife = 56.FG.), B-17G, einige P-38Js und eine A-20G. **23** P-47C vom 335.FS, 4.FG mit 108 Gallon Zusatztribstoffbehälter unterm Rumpf. Die weisse Erken-nungsstreifen und die rote Kokardeumrandung, die für spät 1943 typisch waren, beachten. **24** P-47Ds vom 353.FS, 354.FG mit gelben Motorenhauben. Die dunkelen Scheiben (Schutz gegen die Sonne) vor und hinter der Kanzelhaube beachten! **25** Versuchsweise Anbringung von 20 mm Kanonen unter den Flügeln der P-47 von Col. Frederic C. Gray, Kommandeur der 78.FG, Oktober 1944. **26** Pilot (2nd Lt. Jucheim) und Ober-mechaniker (Staff Sgt. McCord) einer P-47C der 4.FG. **27** Flügplatze könnten mit Stahlplatten innerhalb zwei Wochen erbaut werden. Die Flugzeuge sing P-47Ds vom 404.FS, 371.FG, 1st Tactical Air Force (Provisional). **28** 'Chunky' eine Thunderbolt der 358.FG mit zwei 1,000 lb Bomben und Zusatztreibstoffbehälter. **29** P-47D Thunderbolts vom 81.FS, 50.FG, 9th Air Force inder Normandie. Die Seafire III -Wrack im Hintergrund stammt vom einer der Fleet Air Arm Einheiten, die für Foto-Aufklärungsz eingesetzt wurden. **30** Gelbschnabelige P-51D (44-13926, E2-S) vom 375.FS, 361.FG, 67 Fighter Wing, 8th Air Force.

31 'Sky Bouncer', eine P-51D Mustang vom 375.FS auf Übungseinsatz mit der 91. Bomber Group, Juli 1944. **32** Die schöne Linie der P-51D (hier eine Maschine vom 375.FS) sind von unten, wie hier, klar zu sehen. **33** Fowlmere, 2. März 1945. P-51C, 43-25050 mit Erkennungsbuchstaben – D7 und der roten Seitensteuerfläche des 503.FS, 339.FG, 8th Air Force. **34** Lt. Col. Roy A. Webb, Kommandeur des 374.FS, 361.FG in seiner Mustang. **35** 'Dallas Doll', SX-I, 44-14495, eine P-51D des 352.FS, 353.FG zu Raydon, Dezember 1944. **36** AP-51B des 382.FS, 363.FG mit der Malcolm-Kanzelhaube die die Sicht weit verbesserte. **37** 5E-S 'Elsie 4', eine Mustang des 358.FS, 364.FG, 67th Fighter Wing, 8th Air Force; Honnington, 20. September 1944. **38** Die gelb-schwarz karierte Rumpfspitze (353.FG) hier auf der Maschine vom 352.FS, Dezember 1944 zu sehen. Später kamen noch fünf gelb-schwarze Reihen dazu. **39** YJ-M 'Ginny', eine P-51D des 351.FS, zu Raydon, Januar 1945. Die vergrösserte Rumpfspitaenmarkierung beachten! **40** Eine Mustang vom 383.FG, Honnington, Mai 1945, Mustangs der 8th Air Force mit Raketenabschusseinrichtungen unter den Flügeln kamen nur selton vor.

41 'Fools Paradise IV', eine 9th Air Force Mustang vom 380.FS, 363.FG mit den D-Day Erkennungsstreifen vom Rumpf und von den Flugeloberflächen nur grob entfernt. **42, 43** 'Don Melen' mit Erkennungsbuchstaben LH und die gelbe Seitensteuerfläche des 350.FS, 353.FG. 'Donna Mite' (SX) Lat die schwarze Seitensteuerfläche vom 352.FS der selben Gruppe. **44** Capt. Richard A. Peterson in seiner P-51D vom 364.FS, 357.FG. Capt. Peterson war Flieger-As: ihm wurden 15.5 Luftsiege zugeschrieben. Dieses Bild wurde von einer M-G Stelle einer beschädigten Bomber, die er nach Hause begleitete, gemacht. **45** Bordbesatzung eines 9th Air Force Nachtjagdflugzeuggeschwader vor ihrer P-61 Black Widow. **46** Glanzschwarze P-61 auf einem vorgeschobenen Flugplatz, Frankreich, September 1944.

Farbtafeln

Seite 25 Technical Sergeant. US 8th Air Force im olivgrünen Ausgeh-und Dienstanzug. Die Mütze trägt die Luftwaffenfarbigen Biesen-Orange und Dunkelblau. Dienstgradabzeichen werden auf beiden Armen, das 8th AF Abzeichen nur links getragen. Am linken Unterarm eine Dienststreife (3 Jahre).

Seite 26 (Oben) Spitfire Vb, EN 918 vom 335.FS, 4.FG, Debden, Oktober 1942. Vorschriftsmässigen RAF grau-grüne Tarnfarbenschema. Die Spirale am Propellor, die Rumpfstreife und Erkennungsbuchstaben sind in 'Sky Type S' Farbe. 'AV' heisst 335. Squadron; 'X' das Flugzeug. Die 32 Zoll Kokarden auf den Flügeln sind ohne, die Kokarden zu den Rumpfseiten dagegen mit gelber Umrandung. Dieses Geschwader wurde vom No. 121 (Eagle) Squadron RAF umbenannt.

Seite 26 (Unten) P-51B, 43-24823 vom 362.FS, 357.FG; Leiston, Juni 1944. 'Old Crow' wurde von Capt. Clarence E. Anderson, dessen Siegstafel unterm Kanzel angebracht worden ist, geflogen. Die unangestrichene Kanzelhaube-metallteile beachten! Die schwarzweisse D-Day Erkennungsmarkierungen bestehen aus '18 inch' breite streifen. Falls die Erkennungsbuchstaben auf den weissen Streifen fallen, so haben sie eine schwarze Umrandung. Am Schwanzfloss ist eine '15 inch' weisse Streife noch zu sehen. Zweck dieser Streife war es, Verwechselungen zwischen die Mustang und die Bf109 zu vermeiden. Die rot-gelben Rumpfspitzenmarkierungen bedeuten 357.FG.

Seite 27 Zu beachten sind die Markierungslosen Oberflächen und die mattrote Erkennumgsnummer dieser P-61 Black Widow vom 422. Night fighter Squadron. Vorne, im mattschwarzer Rumpfspitze ist die Radarantenna.

Seiten 28–29 In dieser Lockheed P-38J-10-LO, 42-67825 'Texas Ranger IV' führte Col. Jack S. Jenkins, Kommandeur der 55. Fighter Group, den ersten Jäger-einsatz nach Berlin am 3. März 1944. Die Erkennumgsbuchstaben 'CG' und die weissen Dreiecke an den Schwanzflösse heissen '38.FS'. Innen an den Seitensteuerflächen erscheint die Flugzeugerkennungsbuchstabe 'J'. Die verschiedenen Anbringungsarten der Name an den zwei Rumpfspitzenseiten beachten!

Seite 30 Republic P-47D, 42-28929 vom 405.FS, 371.FG, 9th Air Force. Der Heimatflugplatz für taktische Einsätze März 1945 war Metz-Frescaty, Frankreich. Dieses unangestrichene Flugzeug trägt Rumpfspitze-und Schwanzmarkierungen in 'Insignia Blue' und 'Insignia Red'. Die olivgrünen Sonnenblendescheiben vor-und hinterm Kanzel, sowie die unangewöhnliche Anbringung der Flugzeugerkennungsbuchstabe 'X' halb unterm Schwanz beachten. Die National-kokarde an der Steuerbordflügelunterseite ist extra gross (40 inch Durchmesser) um die schnelle Erkennung zu helfen.

Seite 31 (Oben) Erkennungsfarben der 8th Air Force Jagdeinheiten. A =55.FG, Juli 1944. A1 =343.FS (Buchstaben -CY), A2 =338.FS (Buchstaben -CL), A3 =38.FS (Buchstaben -CG). B =78.FG, Dezember 1944. B1 =84.FS (Buchstaben -WZ), B2 =83.FS (Buchstaben -HL), B3 =82.FS (Buchstaben -MX). C =56.FG, Mai 1944, C1 =63.FS (Buchstaben -UM), C2 =62.FS (Buchstaben -LM), C3 =61.FS (Buchstaben -HV). D =20.FG, Juli 1944. D1 =55.FS (Buchstaben -KI). D2 =79.FS (Buchstaben -MC). D3 =77.FS (Buchstaben -LC).

Seite 31 (unten) Willys $\frac{1}{4}$-ton 4 × 4 Mehrzweckfahrzeug (Jeep) in typischer 'Tracht' (Vorschrifts-und Unvorschriftsmässiger) einer Jagd-Gruppe der 8th Air Force in England.

Seite 32 (Links) Bodenmechaniker der 8th Air Force, 1943–44. Er trägt vorschriftsmässige olivgrüne Arbeitskittel und Mütze, Winter Gummistiefel die mit Metallschnallen versehen sind und eine Schafpelzpiloten-Jacke die er von einem Flieger-Freund 'gewonnen' hat. Die amerikanische Jacke war der RAF Irvin-Jacke sehr ähnlich aber leichter und mit weissem Pelzfutter.

Seite 32 (Rechts) Jagdflieger, 8th Air Force, 1943–44. Er trägt eine olivgrüne Flieger-Jacke rut braunem Pelzkragen und 8th Air Force Schulteremblem. Der Helm und die Levensrettungsweste sind vorschriftsmässig, die Stiefel aber, (vom einer Aufnahme eines Piloten so angezogen) scheinen aus der RAF zu stammen.